Dying to Become One

Kennisha Moffett

Copyright © 2014 Kennisha Moffett

All rights reserved.

ISBN: 0692237755

ISBN-13: 978-0692237755 (MPTM)

DEDICATION

Dedicated to my Lord Jesus who is love, my husband Herb who taught me sacrifice, my children who are my hope, and my mama who gave me tenacity.

Acknowledgements

How do you describe a person who suffers with you, rejoices with you, and lives transparently with you on this journey called life?

Spiritually, Arden Lockwood, is an endless source of wisdom, knowledge, compassion, and integrity. It wasn't until we returned to America that I began to learn of all of her many other talents and accomplishments such as her doctorate, multiple masters degrees, and over twenty years of higher education management and project management experiences.

So, when the time came for me to dust off my old book and get it ready for the world; I knew she was the piece that my book had missed all of these years. In her typical fashion, when I approached her about it, she was ready and available because the Lord had already told her all about it and she was waiting to receive it. Of course the timing couldn't have been worse for us both, as with all great things, but with hard work and dedication, we accomplished our goals. I am eternally grateful to her. On this book she served as my editor, collaborator, advisor, and friend.

With her keen academic eye for formality, instruction, and appropriate perspectives, Arden's contribution to my book will bless all who seek to study, connect, and engage with the material. It was very important to her that the reader not only be moved and given revelation but also motivated to see things from their own perspective. While writing the book, I envision that couples or singles looking for love, would read the book. After my collaboration with Arden, I now understand that it was Gods goal all along to take the limits off. Study groups, congregations, book clubs, or any group of people seeking a growth and transformation in their relationships will find the structure needed to accommodate their discussion as a result of Arden's gift.

Arden has pushed me, encouraged me, and inspired me to dream bigger while holding myself accountable to a daily pursuing greatness. On the journey we've grown closer in our bond and more determined to see each other reach our dreams. I thank you Arden! I honor you! I love you! I will always remember all that you sacrificed and contributed to help me fly.

Kennisha Moffett

Foreword by Herb Moffett

It was a few years ago when Nisha, came into the room and exclaimed, "I have a story to tell. I think I'm going to write a book!" And I responded, "That's great Babe! I think you should." My answer prompted her to question whether she could actually write a book about marriage. I understood her doubts. We had been married for about thirteen years at the time, having more than our share of trials and battles from the very beginning. Together we have confronted just about everything a marriage could confront within the first few years. But by the grace of God and the mercy of Our Lord Jesus Christ we endured, stood for greater, and fought to maintain our life together through challenging life events have torn apart multitudes of other marriages. So, I knew that she was indeed qualified to write *"Dying To Become One"*. Saying so is an understatement. For us to be called upon by so many couples over the years has been an honor and privilege that only God can produce and for that, only He gets the Glory.

Seven years later, I finally had a chance to read this book that she'd spent years laboring over trying to make sure it was transparent, true, and full of revelation for other couples in need of guidance. Through the reading, I was able to step out of the frame of our life and gain great revelations into our marriage. For example, I have come to understand how my entry into Nisha's life was a turning point for her. Before, I didn't understand how she, this beautiful, intelligent, gifted, courageous women, had all but given up on finding a love that would truly love her…brown leaves and all. At the time that we were falling in love, I didn't't know that her heart was opening and accepting for the first time to a transparent and deep love. I too busy experiencing love for the first time myself. Honestly, I thought all beautiful people came from complete, happy homes like mine. Nisha certainly fit the bill as a beautiful person, even once I saw her flaws. It was not until later that I found out where her mindset was concerning marriage and family. I had always believed that when two people fell in love as hard we had, that meant both people were destined to be blissfully and effortlessly happy forever. Oh how I was wrong! But thanks to her Aunt Irene, we were given the greatest key to having a successful, loving, and enduring marriage. Prayer. Inviting God into the middle of our relationship and our relating to each other was the wisest choice we ever made. It was a decision that changed me forever.

    When we met, I was the guy who stayed in the background, never wanting or needing to be the center of attention. In fact, I didn't understand why anyone would want to have the whole room's attention in the first place. But that's exactly who she was then, and that's who she is now. During our college years I was in "The band" and sat in "The chair". Most people in my position developed a taste for the spotlight but I never did. All of that changed after meeting Nisha at Baylor, she brought me out from my own shadow. She is a huge reason for the existence of the man I am today. Every victory that I have experienced as an adult has been a direct result of our first "trip". One weekend she came and grabbed me and simply said, "Come with me. I'm going somewhere and I want you to come with me." I had no idea to where. It wasn't until I saw signs for Dallas/Ft. Worth did I realize she was taking me to her home. That weekend was my first big city experience, the beginning of our life of adventures, and the first fear I overcame. And it was all because of this courageous and fearless woman that God allowed to come into my life.

Two things, despite every one of our mistakes and/or sins, have kept us together. The first is our friendship. From the very beginning we were the best of friends. Friendship was easy for us, it seemed, because we both had learned from childhood how to be friends with the opposite sex from our siblings. In the first months of our new love, we'd just hang out, study together, or get lost watching our favorite TV channel, The Discovery Channel.

Next is our reliance on God for wisdom. We needed much wisdom in order to survive the bridging of our backgrounds.

Has it been perfect? Far from it! Have we remained in perfect love for the last twenty years? Well, that depends on your definition of perfect love. I believe that perfect love is a sacrificial love like Jesus displayed on the cross. So in that regard, it has been perfect. We've both given up our own wills and wants in favor of God's way or the other persons needs.

We knew early on that we didn't know the first thing about being married. We knew that in order for this thing to work, it would take a power greater than either of us possessed. As such, we decided to build our marriage into a triangle of sorts. Each of us, God, Nisha, and myself represented a point on that triangle. God's place was the highest point of the triangle. Our philosophy became that as we each moved closer to God as individuals, the closer we would move towards each other. The middle of the triangle is reserved for our children because one day they would form their own triangle with another.

All in all, our marriage is driven by our desire to die to ourselves, our selfish desires and wants, in favor of meeting the needs and desires of the other. Has this process been done to perfection? By no means is it perfect or where we'd like for it to be but have we have grown day by day…and we're definitely not where we started out. We've grown and all the glory belongs to God.

Over the last two decades, we have walked out *"Dying To Become One"*. I know that this book is going to bless you personally as it has me. I know that after working through the questions in every chapter, your marriage is destined to levels of greatness, intimacy, and transparency that can only come as a gift from the Holy Spirit himself.

Be blessed in your reading and growing!

Herbert R. Moffett, Jr.
Devoted Husband

Foreword By Arden Lockwood

Mrs. Kennisha Moffett is honored to be the loving wife of Herbert Moffett, Jr., with whom she nurtures, trains, and encourages their blessed children. Kennisha marvels at the grace of God as her teens, Jade and Trey, mature into their own God-given and unique gifts. As a family, the Moffetts positively impact contemporary culture for Jesus through entertainment, fashion, media, and the most cutting-edge technologies.

Kennisha is also a world-renowned life coach, mentor, and trainer of leaders in transition. She combines her mother's heart and her business acumen as she ministers truth, life, hope, and accountability to her clients and friends. Whether counseling a boardroom executive, a church pastor, or a single mom, Kennisha's wisdom is always heaven-sent. She may begin with cool sips of God's refreshing grace, but she endeavors to guide each of us into the maturity of our God-ordained destiny as one of God's Mighty Kings and Queens.

As an anointed Prophet of God, Kennisha lives a life of worship, prayer, intercession, and service. Grateful for her personal and intimate home in God's secret place, Kennisha transparently reveals how His mercy and joy strengthen her to overcome life's challenges. As a woman of the Word, Kennisha only says what she hears the Father say and only does what she sees the Father do. As a result of the Father working through this Prophet of God, we witness the miraculous: hearts are healed, minds are renewed, and nations come to a saving knowledge of the Lord Jesus Christ.

I know of where I speak about my amazing friend Nisha, because God has ordained our paths to cross time and time again. In 2005, we were strangers in Bari, Italy, and then we became covenant partners when our paths crossed again in Rome. After spending a weekend together in Basel, Switzerland, Nisha and Herb chose to follow God to France in 2007, where I was ministering in a local congregation. As a result, I lived with the Moffett family as they ministered to my broken heart and as I served as a teacher and translator for their family in my beloved, adoptive home of southern France.

Together with the Lord, each of our families has grown and matured in our divine assignments to serve the Body of Christ. By watching the love, patience, and overcoming nature of each of the Moffetts, I can attest that they are grounded in Jesus and called to minister to their family, friends, and neighbors. I pray that you are blessed by Nisha's personal testimony and her godly wisdom gleaned from a lifetime of knowing Him.

Arden Lockwood, PMP

Table of Contents

Foreword By Arden Lockwood i
Table of Contents iii
Introduction 5
What I Remember 9
What I Saw 17
What I Heard 20
Where I Went 33
Finding Love 44
Learning to Pray Together 54
Overcoming with Prayer 79
Discovering Who You are as "One" 89
Learning to Become "One" 94
Getting Along 97
Creating a Life 109
Sharing: We & Us 119
Learning about Faithfulness 124
Finding Your God-Given Purpose 139
Learning to Practice Humility 171
Learning the Power of Grace and Mercy 178
Postscript 196

Introduction

It's common for young girls to dream of getting married. They imagine their husbands, their perfect children, and their dream home. I never had such dreams. I didn't fantasize about meeting the perfect man and living happily ever after. Instead, my fantasies were filled with dreams of going on long quests during which I'd learn of all of my magical powers. My dreams often included discovering that I was a queen who needed to venture away from the only home I'd known to find and return to my castle. As my dreams matured, the queen became a businesswoman. As a successful entrepreneur, I'd travel the world meeting a variety of characters who'd either help me or attempt to hinder me from achieving riches and whatever my heart desired.

No, my childhood dreams didn't include husbands or children. As a queen, I would explore and conquer other lands. Being royalty, I would be courted by an assortment of suitors, all from well-to-do families. But, like Queen Elizabeth, I would never marry. I would never give my heart away to be crushed, disappointed, or imprisoned. I had experienced these emotions enough from the sideline of my parents' relationship troubles. As they hurt, I would hurt. Not quite understanding the depth of the problem or the circumstances that surrounded their pain, I

Introduction

understood that "marriage" love had inflicted the pain. I understood that they had given all and again they were hurting each other.

And, yet, I'm writing a book about marriage?!? I write this book after almost twenty years of being on a journey with my best friend and husband, Herb. It's a book about our love. It's also about my journey, the journey of a flawed person who made every mistake in love, and yet was blessed with love in spite of myself. I have had to learn how to grow and protect that love.

This book is also about the war that has waged against me and the one I love in the pursuit of what is becoming increasingly rare in our society: becoming "one" with another person in marriage to create a family that casts a bright light into the darkness. It's a light that's strong enough to lead others out of darkness. Our story tells the story of a love that has thrived against the odds for almost two decades. We have been used as a sign by the Lord to help multitudes of other couples that have confidently taken on the pursuit of love.

Now many of you are wondering how I can be so bold as to write a book about marriage when I haven't even been married fifty years. I can be this audacious because I know that most marriages fall apart in the first seven to eight years. Sometimes the failure of unions is reflected in a divorce, but more often it's reflected in a family's dead existence together.

This book is intended to help those of you in the first seven to eight years of marriage. If you've been married longer, our trials, testimonies, and revelations learned may still be a blessing to you and your spouse.

But before I can share the wisdom I have learned throughout the years, I must first return to my childhood to explain what I have overcome and why I am so passionate about sowing into the lives of married people. As I open my heart and my life to you, know that I am praying that you will receive God's revelation, strength, and encouragement from these words from the deepest parts of me.

So, I pray, in the name of Jesus, for you the reader. I pray that our Father in Heaven would reward your search as He did for my family and me. I pray that this book would be a source of inspiration, revelation of what's possible for those who believe and rely on the Lord Jesus, and a catalyst for change.

For this cause, I bow my knee before our Father, whom every family in heaven and on earth is named. I pray that He would grant you, according to the riches of His glory, to be strengthened with power through His Spirit in your inner man, and that our Lord Jesus may dwell in your heart and the hearts of those in your family through faith.

I pray that each of you would be rooted and firmly established in love, so that you may be able to comprehend with all the members of God's family what is the length and width, height and depth of God's love and to know Jesus's love that surpasses knowledge, so you may be filled with all the fullness of God.

Introduction

To God who is able to do above and beyond our most creative prayers or thoughts, according to the power working in you, to Him we give glory in the church and in Jesus, forever! Amen!

Peace to You,
Kennisha Moffett

What I Remember

I expect you are excited to know all of the wise counsel that my husband and I have practiced during our marriage, and I promise I will share that with you. But, first, there is an important principle to understand. In building a solid home for the future, a wise builder inspects the plot of land and double-checks that the foundation will be sure and secure. You may recognize that architects secure permits from authorized people before they are allowed to dig the first hole for a building's footer. The necessity of this step becomes even more crucial the taller or more expansive the building will be.

I find it important to do the same in building relationships, especially one as complex as that as a healthy marriage: turn over some stones, double-check the lay of the land, and ensure that the future development will progress wisely. Therefore, over the next few chapters, I will reflect back on my childhood, my first romance, and how I met my husband, Herb. And while you might find a few of the details under my stones a bit untidy, I promise that Holy Spirit has been a faithful architect in "straightening out" our foundation, and he will do the same for you as you ask him to

What I Remember

help the two of you better understand your pasts and prepare for an amazing future together.

My earliest memories seem to be loaded with very happy moments. My mama was the baby of eight siblings with parents who loved the Lord. As a southern, black, Christian family, we all got to together for every holiday, family reunions, and any other occasion possible. I came from the kind of large extended family that prays together, eats large meals, talks loud, and is always looking for a reason to laugh. My mama was no exception.

When I was a young kid, my mama played with my younger brother and me. She spent many hours talking to us, always allowing us to ask her any question that came to our minds. My brother and I were the Huck Finns of our neighborhood, constantly seeking out our next adventure. My mama encouraged us to explore, as long we followed her rules. Like Huck Finn or Tom Sawyer, however, sometimes our adventures carried us into trouble.

I remember one time when my brother and I were harassing a neighborhood goat that mysteriously got loose and chased us up a tree. We were in that tree for hours. Mama had previously warned us often to leave the goat alone, but we hadn't listened to her wisdom. So, when she found us up the tree, she laughed and didn't bother spanking us because we were already traumatized enough.

Mama's discipline system was clearly understood by all parties involved. She never spanked us before we were talked to for hours, and we were never spanked for anything random. She did a great job of laying down her rules and expectations of us, so that when there was an offense my brother and I already knew that we had willingly disobeyed our mother.

My brother and I also understood the consequences of our disobedience: the spanking process was almost an event at our house. Before justice was served, mama always wanted to know what motivated us to disobey, so we explained why we had broken her rules. As a kid, I couldn't yet value the lesson I was learning in those pre-spanking talks.

Today, however, I recognize that my mother was teaching me to analyze myself, contemplate my actions, and think through my motivations. She taught me to critically think before I act, and to understand that my thinking preceded my actions, followed by the consequences thereafter. Spankings were not random acts from my mother: they were the end result of my willful disobedience to wise rules designed to keep my younger and me brother safe.

As I aged, my mama began to forego the punishment if my analysis and understanding were sound enough during the pre-spanking conversations. As a parent, I now marvel at the patience she harnessed to speak for hours to my brother and me as she sought to train us up wisely. I respect her so much for that patience, now that I recognize how angry, disappointed, or afraid she must have been about our behavior and our safety. My admiration is even higher when I realize how much effort it takes to parent children, especially when my mama was always working so hard outside our home, too.

My childhood memories are full of love, parental support, and adventure. My mama made me feel fearless. My step-dad was also kind. Even though he didn't spend the hours cultivating my young life like my mama did, he was present: kind, but not really engaged.

When I was 12 years old, however, my life changed significantly. At school, I was being bullied during the day, and my mama and step-dad began violently fighting at night. On the rare occasion when my parents were not fighting, I spent restless nights running from horrible things in my dreams. My happy life seemed to change suddenly, and violence and anger opened the door of my heart to feelings of rejection, insecurity, and flight.

Even though my mama couldn't fix her crumbling marriage, she tried to rescue me from my day-time torment by forcing me to stand up to the bullies at school; my mama used the best wisdom she had from her own challenged life of overcoming obstacles. When the bullying continued despite her many attempts to resolve the issue with my teacher and principal, my mama gave me an ultimatum. I will never forget what she said to me: "Nisha, you either fight those bullies or I'll spank you when you get home. That's the deal."

Wow! That was *not* a comfortable set of options for a young girl. Because I believed my mama, I began to cry. I was very afraid of both my mama *and* the bullies. It didn't seem fair that I had to act in this difficult situation.

Recognizing the fear I had of facing my tormenters, my mother continued with her street-smart counsel: "All you have to do is pick one of them, Nisha. Start with the one you think you can beat. Punch her in the face as hard as you can and the other ones will leave you alone." While I may not counsel my own child to take such steps today, I recognize now that my mother was trying—in her own way—to teach me to face my fears and practice being courageous despite the "giants" that try to torment me.

Thankfully, despite my mama's ultimatum, she gave me the grace to find my own strength and timing to face these giants. After a few more weeks of being tormented in class and on the way home by a band of six girls—every day, all day—I finally found my courage. I will never forget it.

I had endured the bullying from the beginning of fifth grade until this moment, the last week of my sixth grade year. I was in my classroom with the gang of six girls as we prepared to go outside. The teacher had just teamed me up with one of my bullies for a three-legged race, which seemed ultimately cruel to me. Didn't my teacher know that my tormenters hated me?!

What I Remember

Anyway, we were supposed to be changing into our tennis shoes for the three-legged race when they attacked me once again. Even though the bullying seemed the same as it had been for the past two years, *I* was not the same person inside, and my attackers were surprised at how I acted that day.

From a place of anger, rage, and fear inside of me, I finally acted on my mama's words that continued to ring in my head. As my race partner shouted hatefully at me, I punched her in the face!

Shocked at my response, the other girls fled, just as my mama said they would.

No one realized that I had just found out that my parents were getting a divorce. They didn't know how angry I was with the drastic changes in my life, and that I needed a place to express my pain. Raging over the demise of my family and my happy childhood, I kept hitting my bully until the teacher pulled me off of her face.

No, violence is not always a wise solution. But, I find it is necessary even as an adult to begin to recognize that there *is* a time to stand firmly and draw on courage even when it feels like all hell is breaking loose. I imagine, on some level, that young David had to fight past tormenters and fears to stand against the giant Goliath in the Bible. I also imagine that young Joshua was terrified to have to lead all of the children of Israel into the Promised Land without the leadership of Moses.

Despite the complexities of dealing with childhood bullies, today I remember my newfound courage that surged through my body after I gained victory over my school bullies. I took this newfound confidence with me into middle school and I never allowed any of my peers to bully me again.

Even then, I wasn't quick to start a fight. I preferred to find a peaceful solution. But, as soon as defending myself became the only option, I engaged to destroy my opponent and any thoughts of future battles.

Today, I still draw on the courage and strength I learned from my mama. At times I have to stand firmly and defend myself against tormenting thoughts of insecurity. At other times, I have to stand and fight to keep my marriage strong. Living as an adult requires courage and strength, but living as a married couple requires even more!

What do you remember?

Maybe your childhood was always peaceful and loving. If so, praise God!

More commonly, however, contemporary childhoods are interspersed or overwhelmed with difficult times that deeply influence how we see our futures and ourselves.

Just as I share reflections from my past in these first few chapters, I invite you to take time and remember the encouraging and the challenging parts of your childhood.

1. What were your happiest childhood memories? How did your family encourage those happy times?

What I Remember

2. Do you remember a time when you felt oppressed on all sides? How was your family involved at that time?
3. Did you have a counselor or advocate during the challenging times? Did you take the advice? How did it turn out?
4. When were you the strongest and most courageous as a child?
5. If you could imagine your childhood differently, what might you have done differently? Why?

What I Saw

Even after I overcame the bullies at school, life at home still tormented me. My mama and step-dad fought incessantly most nights for the next several months, before we moved away from my step-dad. During those last few months together as a family, it was as if I lived with scary strangers at night until my parents came home during the day and life would appear as normal.

As is typical in violently dysfunctional families, however, we never discussed the anger between my parents. Even though my mama would spend hours coaching me and my brother through those pre-spanking learning sessions, no one sat my brother and me down to explain or apologize for the terror we witnessed night after night. It was as if the adults thought it never happened if we didn't talk about it.

My little mind, however, never forgot.

Despite the growing strength and courage I experienced by overcoming the school bullies, fear and helplessness within the dynamics of my family home reinforced how I saw my life and my relationships. Understandably, my unhappy and bullied pre-teen's view of unhealthy relationships took deep root in my heart and mind.

Protecting myself from the emotional turmoil, I determined I would <u>not</u> be dominated or controlled ever again! I would be strong and confident enough to protect myself at school and in my home, rather than allow myself to feel the fear and torment of those years. Unfortunately, this unbalanced thinking dominated my relationships for many years to come.

Even though my youngest years were peaceful and happy at home, my teenage view of marriage and commitment was transformed from sweet moments of pleasure when I compared the kindness of my step-dad to my mama only short time before to a perceived lifetime of hell and chaos because of their nightly fights.

When I considered the thought of marriage, my response was, "Oh no! I don't see *that* in my future." I could not imagine myself entering into an agreement that stripped me of my freedom to fly and explore. I could not see any joy in such a commitment that ultimately would become the chains that bound me to a wall of suffering. I did not want to live a life of continuous torment!

What do you see?

It has taken many years for my vision about marriage and relationships to become more balanced and loving. Through those transitions, it was necessary for me to clearly see where the roots of my fears and emotional barriers originated. What do you see when you look back to your teen years?

1. Can you envision a time when your perception about marriage and relationships shifted? What were the circumstances that changed your point of view? Was it a dramatic shift, or just a little nudge to the more positive or more negative view of lifelong relationships?
2. Looking back, do you believe you accurately saw the whole picture? Or, is it possible that you were only able to process a portion of the truth because of the circumstances of the situation?
3. How do you see marriage and relationships today?
4. If you were to speak to that younger version of yourself today about love and marriage, what different perspective would you share?

What I Heard

While grieving the loss of her marriage, my mama—as a single mother—barely kept things together for my brother and me. Even though she worked three jobs, we had times without a phone or utilities. While she worked, my brother and I were responsible for ourselves to do well at school and manage the house. Looking back, my childhood ended when mama's divorce ended.

Without any transition, I became responsible for adult household tasks that had previously been just childhood chores. As a result of this pressure—and the stiff potential consequences for disappointing my mother—my life became full-time work. I did *not* want to experience "the wrath of mama" if she came home tired from her multiple jobs to find I had been disobedient to her wishes!

Unfortunately, the shift to adult responsibilities also shattered my relationship with my younger brother. While we had been close with our neighborhood adventures as young children, we became near enemies when we were alone together most days. Both of us were afraid and insecure about the changing patterns of our family, but we didn't know how to communicate the hurts or disappointments. So, like children, we began to fight over everything, especially as I struggled to act responsibly as the older sister: I was a child, myself, and I was ill equipped to manage so much change.

This season was a hard, depressing time in the lives of my mama, my brother, and me: none of us knew how to best handle the financial and emotional turmoil in which we lived. Unfortunately, it seemed that a wedge of division was driven between my brother and me that lasted for over a decade.

Looking back, I understand that my mama did the best she knew how in those difficult circumstances as a single mother of two children. Even still, I now recognize that my needs for stability, support, and love were suddenly unfulfilled. I felt I had lost my parents, my childhood, *and* my brother who had once been my best friend and stabilizing force during the challenges of the divorce.

It was during these years that I fell in love with The Cosby Show television series. At night, I fantasized about waking up and discovering that I had been with my "real" Cosby family all along, and that the rest had been a bad nightmare. Each day, however, I rose to find that my world—like my young heart—was still broken. As a result of the stark contrast between my imagined hopes and my unstable reality, I became more angry and desperate to create my own world far away from home.

By the time that I was old enough to start having relationships outside of my family, I had a strong mistrust and fear of people. I also had no real desires for romantic love. I enjoyed people, but I purposely kept my relationships shallow: it was emotionally safer that way.

As soon as someone got on my nerves, I would throw them away. I did maintain a few female friends, but even those relationships were not sustained very well, because I feared needing anyone outside of God and myself. How could I trust another person, when I felt my own parents had abandoned me?

I quickly learned that I preferred males as friends, but not as boyfriends. When I limited my relationships with men as friends, the fear of a boyfriend's hurt or emotional imprisonment couldn't rule the relationship. I was free to be me, unguarded and without reservations or expectations. At least, this is how my teenaged-self rationalized my shallow relationships.

In contrast to the publicly shallow Nisha that I had become, I was actually deepening my private relationship with God. During those years of gasping for the air of freedom, smelling glimpses of peace, and seeing small glimmers of hope, I found a place of escape in him. While being bullied at school and watching my family fall apart, I found refuge in my prayers to the Lord.

At the same time, I had a wonderful friend in Peter. He was the only friend with whom I could talk about praying and hearing from God. All my other friends thought that church and prayer was something your parents made you do and that it wasn't to be taken seriously. But not me and Peter: we always knew God was real, and we became fast friends at church. On the outside, Peter and I were both popular, cool kids always in control, but we were a safe haven for each other's secrets of the difficulties in our homes.

I could talk to Peter about everything: about my parents fighting, about my fears and fantasies, about how the Lord spoke with me, and about the visions I began to have. Peter, who has since become a successful minister, was blessed of the Lord even then to be wise beyond his years.

When I would tell Peter I could hear God talking to me, he simply asked, "What did he say?"

This little sign of acceptance, safety, and encouragement changed my life. I am so thankful today for the kindness and graciousness that Peter offered to my young, broken heart as I was learning to hear from God.

One method God used to train me to hear him better was through my involvement at church. Despite my mama's work schedule, she was consistent to send my brother and me to a good Baptist church twice a week, just as she had been raised. My brother and I went to Bible Study, Sunday School, and Children's Church service every week. Church was great and I learned a lot. The church leadership and activities taught me about the Bible, morality, and Christian service to other people. At church, I listened with passion. Struggling to learn how to overcome my

What I Heard

life's burdens and grief, I hoped that I would hear God through his word and often I did.

At age eleven, I gave my life to Christ because of what I heard through my heart. My external life didn't change immediately, but internally I was a new person. I heard Jesus speak to me at night or anytime when I was quiet. I could feel his presence near me when I was alone. The Lord became my dad and my friend, especially during the challenges of living in a dysfunctional family.

God regularly spoke to me and I recognized him, but I was not yet mature or confident enough to clearly discern his voice from my own. But, like a thirsty child, I ran towards him with all the hope and faith I could find. The Lord had become real to me since I was very little in my large, loving, Christian, extended family. He had my heart and I always felt free to be transparent with him. While my immediate family and the school bullies brought me torment, God always represented peace and hope to me: I did not feel fearful when I spoke with God.

Because of my family struggles, I learned to speak more clearly with God during a lot of alone time during my teenage years. I learned that conversation with a friend also requires a lot of listening. Because I was so desperate for acceptance and love, I cried out to God without yet knowing to listen. Thankfully, God was graceful, as he overlooked my ignorance and found a way to train me to communicate more maturely; he desires to speak with all people, no matter how old or how young they are. As I learned to listen to him even more, I continued to grow in my discernment of spiritual things.

What I Heard

What do you hear?

Learning to hear from God, despite the challenges of my life, is the most valuable lesson I have ever experienced. Take a few moments and consider what you have heard from your past.

1. Who was the most encouraging and accepting friend you had? What did s/he say that made you feel safe?
2. Where did you enjoy going as a child? Were you involved in a church, scouts, or some other social organization? What did you hear at those gatherings?
3. Do you remember ever wondering if God existed as you looked at the night sky or the vastness of a beach?
4. Have you ever heard how much God loves you? He loves you so much, and he wants to talk with you. Will you hear his voice?

Learning how to hear from God

For I do not speak of myself, but from the Father who sent me and commanded me what I should say and what I should speak. And I know that [to obey] his command is life everlasting. Therefore, <u>whatever I speak is just as the Father tells me to speak.</u>" John 12:49-50

Like any good parent, God desires to speak with all of His children. His word says that His sheep know His voice and another voice they will not follow (John10:27). My hunger to hear from the Lord clearly begins with this scripture and ends with Jesus's words that He only did what he saw and heard the Father say (John5:19).

As a child, I learned and believed that if Jesus could hear and receive instructions from God then I could, too.

So, without much effort, I did hear God clearly. But, as I aged and the cares of the world grew, I struggled to hear him as clearly. In desperation, I asked the Lord to teach me how to hear from him when all hell is breaking loose, and he did.

I have since taught my children and countless others the following practical steps.

STEP 1: *Tune Your Ears to Hear*

For 30 days, set aside an hour (or at least 30 minutes) of your day for fellowship with God. During that time, speak only to ask God to teach you how to hear from him. Then listen. It's best to have a journal to write down what you hear. This exercise requires total silence.

Think about it. If God is god of all and all knowing, why do we do most of the talking during our prayer times? Even as I speak to my children, after I allow them to express themselves, they have been trained to listen as I speak. It's in the listening that they gain wisdom and guidance for their lives. I believe it's also a sign of respect and humility when we submit our ears to the Lord.

The Lord is a gentleman, so he won't force us to listen. He requires us train our spiritual ears to be still in order to hear his still small voice. So, be quiet. Also, be persistent. If you don't hear him the first day, don't quit. Stay the course. God is faithful and he will reward your diligence and your desire to commune with him.

What I Heard

STEP 2: Grow Your Faith to Hear From Him
So faith comes by hearing, and hearing by the word of God. Romans 10:17

For years, I feared telling people that I heard God speaking to me, because most people I knew just simply would not have believed me. This form of doubt among Christians is common. Despite, the overwhelming proof that God has talked to man all throughout the Old and New Testament, many Christians still believe that God won't speak to them.

I encourage you to not miss out on a thriving relationship with the Father for any reason. He wants to speak with you. His desire is to have an intimate relationship with all of his children. It is possible to overcome your doubts. Simply feed your faith in this area. Faith comes by hearing the word. So, read scriptures, out loud, that will grow your faith. Read them daily, post them around your house, and meditate on them.

Here are a few scriptures to get you started, but there are many more. Seek them out.

For all who are led by the Spirit of God are children of God. Romans 8:14

Roll your works upon the Lord [commit and trust them wholly to Him; He will cause your thoughts to become agreeable to His will, and] so shall your plans be established and succeed" Proverbs 16:3

"...and the sheep follow Him, for they know His voice. Yet they will by no means follow a stranger, but will flee from him, for they do not know the voice of strangers." John 10:4-5

Your ears shall hear a word behind you, saying, "This is the way, walk in it," Whenever you turn to the right hand or whenever you turn to the left." Isaiah 30:21

Howbeit when he, the Spirit of truth, is come, he will guide you into all truth: for he shall not speak of himself; but whatsoever he shall hear, [that] shall he speak: and he will shew you things to come. John 16:13

Whoever belongs to God hears what God says. The reason you do not hear is that you do not belong to God. John 8:47

What I teach comes from the One who sent me. Anyone who wants to do his will can test this teaching and know whether it's from God or whether I'm making it up. A person making things up tries to make himself look good. But someone trying to honor the one who sent him sticks to the facts and doesn't tamper with reality. John 10:17-18 (The Message)

So how can you know whether you're hearing the voice of God?

The Bible gives us basic keys or filters through which every possible leading should be judged. We are to carefully examine the

What I Heard

thoughts and intentions of our hearts – and the words of godly people who may have influence on us by their words and actions – through the use of these keys:

All Scripture is given by inspiration of God, and is profitable for doctrine, for reproof, for correction, for instruction in righteousness, that the man of God may be complete, thoroughly equipped for every good work. II Timothy 3:16-17

For this is the covenant that I will make with the house of Israel after those days, says the Lord: I will put my laws into their minds, and I will write them on their hearts. and I will be their God, and they shall be my people. And they shall not teach everyone his fellow citizen, and everyone his brother, saying, 'know the Lord,' for all will know Me, from the least to the greatest of them. Hebrews 8:10-11

Do not quench the Spirit; do not despise prophetic utterances. But examine everything carefully; hold fast to that which is good. I Thessalonians 5:19-21 Where no counsel is, the people fall: but in the multitude of counselors there is safety. Proverbs 11:14

By the mouth of two or three witnesses every fact may be confirmed. Matthew 18:16

Let the peace of Christ rule in your hearts, to which indeed you were called in one body; and be thankful. Colossians 3:15

STEP 3: Get to Know "The Word" from Your Bible

In the beginning was the Word, and the Word was with God, and the Word was God. John 1:1

The more I get to know the Lord, the more this scripture grows in its importance. It is proof that God existed and far exceeds the boundaries of his written word, the Bible. Think about it. Before it was written, men like Abraham and Job spoke with him. They spoke with "The Word." I am certain that even they struggled to some degree to make sense of it all.

Today we are fortunate that the Lord has left us a written account of his experiences with humanity and his divine inspiration. From the Bible, we can learn much about our Father in Heaven, his character, his ways, and his decrees throughout time. It's a short cut to intimacy with him after we accept his son Jesus as our Lord and savior.

One of the most exciting aspects of the Bible is that we can hear his voice when we spend time in Bible study and quiet contemplation of his Word. The more time we spend intimately with God and his Word, the easier it is to recognize his voice and his leading in our lives. Employees at a bank are trained to recognize counterfeits by studying genuine money so closely that it is easy to spot a fake. We should be so familiar with God's Word that when someone speaks error to us, it is clear that it is not of God.

What I Heard

While God *could* speak audibly to people today, He speaks primarily through his written Word and directly to our spirits. Sometimes God's leading can come through the Holy Spirit, through our consciences, through circumstances, and through the exhortations of other people. By comparing what we hear to the truth of scripture, we can learn to recognize God's voice.

I encourage you to study your Bible to learn about God. We've all done character studies on great men and women of the Bible, but have you done one on God? What does the Bible teach you about him?

Dying to Become One

Where I Went

As I matured with God during my teen years, I still yearned to stay in control of my life and I eventually escaped my mama's home to go to college. I attended a prestigious, historically white, Baptist university. I wasn't afraid or intimidated despite my economically challenged, black upbringing, because I was free! Without looking back, I left everything that I had ever known to be alone on my own terms.

Life in college was everything I hoped it would be, even from the start. Despite my financial struggles, I never once considered being anywhere else. Unlike high school, many suitors also appeared when I stepped on campus. I soon had many male friends who clearly understood that male-female friendships did not have to be sexual. I soon learned how deeply repulsed the diverse cultural populations on the Baptist campus were to the state of "loose" dating, and I felt safe.

I simply adored life at Baylor University. It was so far away from pain and suffering that I rarely went home during my first few years of college. Instead, I worked tirelessly at achieving my dreams of academic success that could propel me into international business fortunes. By focusing on my future, I imagined I could forget my hurtful past.

Just as I had thrown away inconvenient high school relationships, I attempted to dismiss my own parents like a dirty rag. Unconditional love, however, cannot be discarded or ignored. Like the fighter that she is, my mama stood strong and battled to maintain our ties with one another, even against my own stubborn tactics. She forced her way into my campus life in fights, unannounced visits, or whatever she had to do to stay in my life.

Looking back, I love my mama immensely for her tenacity! She held on to me in love and in prayer as she waited out the storm of my immature neglect. At the time I was angered at my mama's "interference" in my life, because I could not recognize her actions as those of a loving parent. Despite the hurt I caused her as I tried to protect my wounded heart as a young college student, my mama refused to let go of me like my superficial friends had done.

At college, I was becoming all that my mama hoped I would be: strong, independent, and connected to the Lord. She was proud of me and I could feel it despite our physical distance and my emotional stonewalling. While her consistent love was unable to change the condition of my barricaded heart for many years, my mama's love was like water dripping endlessly on stone so that it eventually strips away layers of rock. Today, I seek to be the kind of mother who gives her children this kind of sacrificial, selfless love that grounds them while they find their own way in life.

For most of my college years, I steered clear of true love. I had infatuations, crushes, and flings, but no one took the place of my three cherished treasures: 1) the need for freedom, 2) my relationship with the Lord, and 3) the attainment of riches which was riding in the passenger seat as freedom drove the car. I wish I could say that the Lord was at least in the car, but it took several more years for me to get that revelation. During those years, I was a rebellious daughter to an awesome heavenly Father.

College was a bubble of endless fun and joy for me. I began to forget that some people could be cruel and incapable of real love. I began to crave emotional and physical intimacy, but I feared fulfilling this desire. What if it were to go wrong, so that I might have to see my ex-boyfriend on campus with another woman? I refused to put myself in that position, so I rationalized that I needed to wait on finding true love.

But what about casual sex?

I now understand that when you speak things contrary to God's will for your life, the enemy can fulfill your words. He seeks constantly whom he can devour and, unfortunately, our words can give him inside information on how to set the trap. And I made my words very clear for the enemy to set up a trap for me.

I began to tell my friends that I was lonely and wanted to have sex. I wasn't lonely for companionship, because I had plenty of male and female friends. I even had many willing suitors at Baylor, but I justified that I didn't want to be entangled physically on the campus of a Baptist university.

I imagined that my college life should stay "pure," even if I engaged in pre-marital sex. "Pure." What a joke! Through the twisted thinking of my youthful hormones and my stony heart, I equated purity with keeping my public image free from outside judgment. I wanted to "do dirt," as long as it was away from my Christian community that wouldn't condone these behaviors. Basically, I wanted to be sexually intimate with someone beyond the walls of my proper, prestigious, white, Baptist university world.

The enemy fulfilled my evil desires more quickly than I could imagine with a guy who was fun, exciting, and wasn't working hard to date me. He moved effortlessly and gracefully, and he was dangerous to my wall of barricaded protection.

He was a male version of me!?

This revelation frightened me. If he were truly like me, I knew he couldn't be trusted. But my youthful lusts wanted to trust him. In hindsight, I should have stopped and prayed before proceeding with that relationship. Frankly, however, I was too busy "getting to know him" to pray.

Despite all the warning sirens to both my head and my heart, I jumped in with both feet.

Lust was in control!

We had a whirlwind romance that lasted for the spring in the dark corners away from the light of the Baylor campus. By the summer, however, my heart was betrayed like never before and my dreams were in jeopardy. Not only was my lover as superficial and dangerous as I had feared, he was shameless and irresponsible. We both were. I had chosen the destructive path to temporary passion and been betrayed by it. The climax of this nightmare came with the murder of the innocent and the death of my peace for a time.

I was a wreck, and I returned to school even more broken and alone than I had been through all of my family's dysfunctions. I grieved for a year, gained sixty pounds, and barely passed my classes. When I slept, I had dreams of the child I would never hold on this earth. I was haunted with visions of the child while I sat in church or attended class at the Christian university.

I didn't understand at the time that the enemy was infiltrating my shame and guilt to bombard me even further into darkness. I carried so much shame that I thought I *wanted* to be depressed and isolated. Just as I had been so focused on my own lustful choices that I ignored my wiser options, I was too busy punishing myself to notice the enemy's persistence in my thoughts as he drug me deeper into depression.

I believe it was a miracle that I was still going to class despite the abortion, the depression, and the physical and emotional turmoil I was experiencing. But something inside me was pushing me forward despite my circumstances. At the time, I could only imagine that it was my big dream for freedom and prosperity that enabled me to keep going through the motions.

"I can't quit now," is what I told myself.

In hindsight, I was drawing on the tenacity and courage that I had learned from my mama when I overtook the school bullies and fears that had oppressed me. I also see now that God's still small voice must have been speaking words of life and hope into my desperate heart. He had never planned for me to experience the devastation of that horrible relationship, but he had not been surprised.

God had already planted his word into my heart during all those bus trips to and from that wonderful Baptist church. He had already revealed himself to me as a good and faithful dad and friend who will hold me and speak with me when I allow myself to hear his voice. And he never did leave me, despite the barriers I had built so that I could follow my youthful lusts.

God is always faithful, especially in the darkest of circumstances.

One day, after walking in total darkness for about a year, the Lord sent me a voice of hope. Mrs. Pearl had been my boss on campus for several years as I served on the leadership staff of several student organizations before my illicit affair. She had pushed me towards excellence, rebuked me when I was slacking in my classes, corrected some of my thinking, and praised me when I did well. Mrs. Pearl was my friend and my surrogate mother. She was a strong tower to me when I was a student at Baylor and she continues to be a valuable mentor to me to this day.

As anyone knows who has walked in deep sin, I imagined I was doing a good job of hiding my spiritual, emotional, and physical conditions from Mrs. Pearl. Whenever we had a meeting together, I displayed my best joy, smiles, and positive attitude. I didn't know at the time that Mrs. Pearl was reading my eyes *and* my spirit. She had already learned much more about the wisdom of God and how to hear him for the people around her than I had ever imagined possible. God is big!

One day, Mrs. Pearl stopped me as I was walking through the Student Union. She pointed her finger in my face and said, "I don't know what happened to you last summer, but God said that he forgave you. Now forgive yourself."

That's all she said for several minutes as she watched buckets of tears stream down my face.

Just before she walked away, Mrs. Pearl said, "Kennisha, you're better than this. Return to us. I miss you."

Through the words of Mrs. Pearl, the healing power of God's forgiveness washed over me like rain does in a barren land. I awoke from my spiritual stupor and rededicated myself to God, endeavoring to go on with my life. I took off my proverbial sackcloth and ashes and returned to the land of the living!

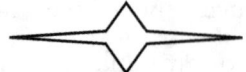

After I returned to myself, I soon learned that Mrs. Pearl's words were completely true: I was missed! All of my friends, church members, and associates mentioned to me, in their own ways, that I was a source of joy in their lives. They were grateful that I had returned to their activities. I had never previously been able to see that I was touching so many lives, or that my absence would matter. Just as I had been so quick in dismissing "inconvenient" people from my own life, I had imagined that other people would dismiss me just as quickly.

I still remember the lessons I learned from those complicated and human experiences as a student looking for freedom at Baylor. I clarified a great deal about myself, what I was attracted to, and what I truly wanted out of life. I needed God more than the freedom to have sex. I needed acceptance and community even more than independence. And I needed God's grace and mercy more than anything else.

I also learned a great deal about deception. Those echoing words of rejection, fear, and abandonment had been lying to me all along. I had value: to Mrs. Pearl, to my friends and colleagues, and to myself and my family.

Similarly, where I had once judged my mama for her failings, I had grace to give instead of judgment. I understood better the power of deceit and lust. I also realized that without

Christ in the center of every thought, no person can withstand the wiles of the enemy.

Because of my broken and isolated experiences, I also began to desire a reconnection with my parents. I imagined a new kind of relationship with my human parents in which I could learn to accept them for who they were instead of who I thought they should be. This journey of healing within my family took many years, but I started down that new road of grace and humility after I saw my own humanity as that formerly broken Baylor student who was loved and restored by God through the strength and wisdom of Mrs. Pearl.

Storing away those lessons in my backpack of life, I started a new phase of my life.

Where did you go?

I thank you for honoring my past, including the unwise choices I have made. Of course I wish I had been wiser, but I can't change them now, can I? But those choices and my responses to them have shaped who I am today: a peaceful, godly woman who believes she is to share her life and her growing wisdom with young couples. Because I have learned to trust God's ways better than my own, I am willing to put myself "out there" if my past and my present can serve as an encouragement to other people.

I invite each of you to take some time and look back over your own pasts and share the highlights and lowlights with God. I recognize that these questions might touch some very sensitive spots in your heart. I also know from experience that learning to look back on my past and allow God's light to shine truth into it heals all kinds of wounds and disappointments. It might be uncomfortable in the short-term, but I believe that you are reading this book today because you are ready and willing to strengthen your foundation as a child of God so that you and your partner can build a strong home for a lifetime of true love.

As I prayed in the Introduction, I believe God will bring light and understanding to you. I also trust that He has already placed wise and loving mentors in your path with whom you can counsel if you have questions about the emotions you might experience during our journey together. But let me pray this over you now:

Dying to Become One

Dear Father,

I come to you in the Name of Jesus on behalf of this glorious couple who is seeking your face. I ask you to support them, nurture them, and clarify their thoughts as they look back on the paths they have chosen to walk in their lives. Help them to truly receive more of the peace that passes all understanding and Holy Spirit's comfort. You promised, Father, that you would never leave them nor forsake them. And I know that you always keep your promises. And, as Mrs. Pearl told me, "You are forgiven. Now forgive yourself."

In all of the Father's love,
Kennisha

Finding Love

After my restoration to my Baylor community, I spent my junior year getting my life back on track, making restitution for my sins, and learning to live a more sanctified life. Overall it was good because God's grace overcame my sinful and willful choices such that he gave me another year at Baylor, covered me financially despite my constant struggles, and drew me closer to him. It was all good!

The Lord even sent me wonderful Christian friends to surround me and to whom I could stay accountable. While I still enjoyed socializing and throwing parties, I became more serious about setting my plans for after college. Actually, my closest friends began to graduate and leave the campus, and I was busier than ever before as I prepared for graduation, worked to pay my bills, and focused myself on keeping my life in better order.

I returned to enjoying my male friends while more wisely keeping my own heart guarded. It was easy to let my male friends know more plainly of my intentions concerning them, after all that I had come through. After surviving such a physical and emotional tragedy, I even began to dream of real love. My ex-lover contacted me several times, but I was more grounded and I finally trusted my heart and mind regarding his worthless and deceiving love. All my ex-lover could offer was a roller coaster ride that I had no plans of re-entering. My view of what made a good man had finally matured.

As my view of myself and relationships evolved, I realized that I had previously only considered dating guys who were not interested in real love. I was attracting what I had become: gorgeous, charming, well dressed, full of personality, and shallow of heart. As I matured, I began to desire a family guy who really loved God. I realized that the flirtatious leader of a pack wasn't always the brain of the operation. Previously, I had underestimated the quiet, humble spirit of the Lord that exists in some of the wisest leaders.

In my senior year at Baylor, I began to dream of having a family. I imagined honoring God for his forgiveness by being successful in love. Desiring to prove to God that his decision to spare my life was not going to be forgotten, I would wait for God to bring me true love. I would recognize it not by its charm, or sweet smell, or even great looks. Instead, I would recognize true, God-sent love by its fruit: joy, peace, kindness, gentleness, faithfulness, and generosity.

Setting my sights for such noble love, I prepared myself for the possibility of waiting many years. Surprisingly, however, love was already in my camp; I just hadn't noticed him before.

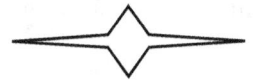

Finding Love

Herb was already among my group of friends, but he was typically reading a book or saying only a few words when we would get together. He was not a suitor or even a close friend; Herb was a friend of a friend. He was the quiet, wise, humble man that I actually knew very well. We worked on several committees together, attended the same parties, sang in the same choirs, ate in the same cafes, and studied at the same Business School. We passed each other every day. I mean *all* day, every day.

After years of working, partying, singing, eating, and studying with Herb at Baylor, I finally *saw* him. And he was gorgeous from the inside out! Where I had previously not recognized Herb for his strong character and noble traits because he wasn't the social group leader, I suddenly recognized the love of God in every aspect of his life. I had matured enough to recognize a quality man from a boy.

I was learning to love Herb as God loved him.

Looking back, I know that God had always envisioned Herb and me together. We became quick friends, once I finally focused my attention on Herb. I realized I wanted to be with him forever. He was intelligent, joyful, and kind. Yet, because of my barricaded heart, my family relationships, and my erroneous perspectives, I struggled with our relationship.

The hardest part was that when I looked at Herb I saw two different guys. Sometimes, I saw the bookworm of a guy with bad skin and poor taste in clothes that I had always ignored because he wasn't as socially adept as I was. At other times, I saw an extremely handsome and mighty man of God who I knew was my future husband. Herb was someone whom I respected, but no dating service in the world would have paired us together. I called him my "diamond in the rough."

On one hand, Herb reminded me of the strengths I associated with my philandering and irresponsible dad: intelligent and conversational, but also always interested in my opinion. Herb was also humble and funny like George Carlin, Lewis Black, or any of the other intellectual comedians who I never watched. As a musician, Herb was also much more of a creative thinker than I was used to. But, mostly, he was fun to be around!

On the other hand, Herb was vastly different from anyone I had ever entertained, and my entire world knew it. My mama asked me if I really liked him. My church family questioned if I was serious about him. No one, not even me, could believe that I had fallen for someone so different.

All of these doubts from other people reinforced my own fears about our relationship. I was afraid of having my insecure heart broken again, and I definitely didn't want to appear uncool or foolish around my glamorous friends. I rationalized that I would keep my thoughts about how great Herb was to myself, attempting to hide my emotions from him and everyone else. If Herb were truly God-sent, then I would wait for God's love to manifest itself in the proper timing.

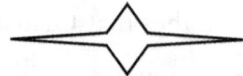

Even as we dated, I realized that Herb was completely unique from anyone else. Our dates were more productive and fun than romantic. We often studied at the library before continuing our studies at the local Denny's restaurant. We even studied when we had picnics at campus! And, yet, on the weekends we veered closer to my comfort zone of fraternity parties and my popular circle of friends: the world of "cool kids" as Herb described it.

But exposing our relationship to the public was a challenge for me for many reasons. Herb was more of a bookworm than a socialite, so I struggled with my own issues and expectations. Delighted to be in my company, however, Herb wanted *everyone* on campus to know we were a couple. But I wasn't so sure.

Not only had I had never been one for public affection, but I had established my own rule that I didn't date people on the campus. Looking back, I am sure that my mama's voice and her consequences of breaking the rules were echoing in my mind. In addition, the whole concept of long-term commitment and relationship success still seemed so foreign to me because of my parents' failed marriages; my own emotional barricades and failed forays into love did not strengthen my forecast for success with Herb.

How was it possible that Herb could seem so perfect and God-sent, and yet I was so conflicted? How was it that he could be so kind and patient, and at times I just wanted to run away from him? And how was it possible that I could have to feel so out of control if Herb was truly to be my future husband who would support my dreams of freedom, travel, and prosperity?

I really didn't understand it all!

By the summer, our spring love had become serious—even more serious than I had realized. Instead of going to the library, one night, Herb took me to a romantic bridge in the middle of a park. Crossing a beautiful river, the bridge was especially popular with couples.

I was surprised when Herb unexpectedly asked me to marry him that night on the bridge. I should have been happy, but the unscheduled words brought back a flood of painful memories and personal declarations about love, family, and marriage. I was the girl who said I would never have a family. Herb didn't know that I had already killed my unborn child, or that I had had three fathers, or that my home life was still pretty messed up.

Even though I was honored by Herb's proposal, I refused to take it seriously. How could I? With my emotional and family past, I believed I wasn't marriage material. I knew I wasn't good enough to marry Herb.

Finding Love

    I was very confused. My heart invited his proposal because I loved him more than I ever imagined I could love someone, but my mind listened to the voices of all of my past issues. The enemy played his part, too. He reminded me of all of my mistakes, my broken family, and my fears. He also threatened me with doubts about Herb's love for me.

    All I could clearly hear that night was: "Your own dad doesn't want you. Why would Herb truly want you? He'll probably leave, too."

    This was before I knew how to rebuke the negative voices out of my mind, so I was often plagued day and night with crazy thoughts and images. Not knowing how to share these attacks, I hid these thoughts from Herb by simply making light of his proposal.

    Looking back, I am sure I challenged even Herb's tender heart that night as he insisted that he was very serious about marrying me. My own insecurities and doubts, however, wouldn't let me truly embrace the God-sent love to be my future husband as we stood on that beautiful bridge in the park.

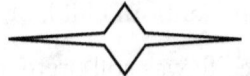

    Wanting to learn to love and to trust Herb completely, I went to God in prayer. I asked him to help me to know what was real and if Herb really loved me. About a week after Herb's proposal, I went to bed and had a vision or a dream; I'm still not sure.

Dying to Become One

In the dream, my cousin who had been brutally murder at 16 years old visited me. He and I had always had a fun relationship and this visit was the same. It seemed like we laughed and talked for hours before he brought up the subject of Herb.

"Cuz, you should marry Herb. He really loves you, and he's a good man."

My cousin's words startled me into remembering that he had been killed years ago. So, I responded, "David, you're dead."

I awoke seconds later. David was gone, but his words about Herb remained in my heart. And God's peace rested there, too.

As a kid, I had often had visions and dreams from God. I had seen more things than I ever cared to admit, but this was the first time I had seen a dead relative in my dreams. Yet, I remember feeling warm and full of joy when I woke up. I'm not sure what I experienced, but it sure felt good. I never felt fear!

I wanted to share my dream with Herb, but I hadn't yet told him that I had strange dreams, just as I hadn't yet told him about my three dads and my crazy family past. How do you learn to trust someone enough to share those deep parts of yourself?

Just as my young friend Peter had been my safe haven when I had learned to hear from God, my grandmother had been the one safe person with whom I had mentioned that I had crazy dreams. Casually, I had just told her that I see things.

Finding Love

"I do, too, honey," was her simple reply. Knowing that at least one person could relate was more than enough to settle my nervousness.

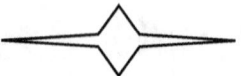

I had told God that I would wait until he sent me my future husband. I never imagined that the quiet bookworm whom I'd known for years could be him, but Herb Moffett's patient love, gentle heart, and glorious spirit seemed to fill a void that had always been in my life. With the odd, but comforting words of a favorite, dead cousin ringing in my ears, I finally accepted Herb's proposal to be his wife!

Once Herb and I got engaged we enjoyed every moment we could spare of our summer break together.

At that time, I underestimated how much my life was about to change. I had no way of knowing the journey that our love would create. I didn't know that I was about to discover, create, and become real love. I was about to become "one" with my lifelong partner and begin a life of ups and downs that have brought me to the writing of this book about marriage.

I never saw it coming!

Finding Love

So, despite the heartache and disappointments of the first twenty years of my life, I finally found love in the most hidden corner of a Baylor campus. Before we continue with what other

Dying to Become One

lessons Herb and I have learned about being a healthy couple, take some time to remember how the two of you came to find one another.

1. How did you and your current partner come together?
2. Were you confident that the two of you should marry? Or did you have some unanswered questions tugging at your heart or mind?
3. Have you been able to identify and share your darkest fears and your highest hopes with each other? If not, why not? Are you ready to start sharing them now?

Finding Love

Learning to Pray Together

After Herb and I were engaged, I constantly prayed for wisdom and direction because I knew it was a serious thing for the two of us, barely even twenty years old would be planning to marry. I prayed to see the truth from lies as well as to understand God's timing.

I prayed to remain stable in my faculties: even though I believed that love at first sight was possible, I never thought it would happen to me. I was especially afraid of what would happen with my marriage to Herb, because I had moved so quickly into my recent affair without thinking and praying about it. Had I made a mistake agreeing to marry Herb, I wondered.

Herb, however, seemed so steady and unmovable about all of it. He didn't have the fears that I had. I worried because we didn't have the finances to get married, we were both seniors in college, and our love was too new to predict all of the other risks we would face. But what fool in love can logically calculate everything?

I am so grateful that Jesus's love for me is more than just logical. I mean, seriously, he had to die so we could live...where is the human logic in that? Dying for a whole world, most of who didn't even know he had arrived in the first place? And yet, Jesus gladly did it.

I don't believe love always makes sense, then or now, but I was still cautious. By all rights, I was an adult. I had been responsible for myself for many years by the time Herb and I met. I had already been financially responsible for myself in college, because my parents had never been in a financial position to provide for my education or living expenses. Of course, my mama helped in any way she could, but the load was still mine.

As a single woman, I worked, went to class, studied, and played...like any adult would. Focused on my goal of graduating, I paid my rent, living expenses, and tuition with loans, grants, and financial aid, while studying enough in my free time to get decent grades. I had a successful routine to achieve my goals!

When I met Herb, I was only a year away from graduation, so my thoughts were constantly on my dream of being a queen free to do as I pleased. For a while, I regretted accepting Herb's proposal for marriage before we talked about all of my dreams; I was torn about how marriage would shift my independence and my priorities. I was also uncomfortable about how married life would impact my ability to independently manage all of my bills as I had done for years. It seemed so irrational to think of marriage before graduation!

Learning to Pray Together

Outside of my closest circle of friends and family, many people may not have known of my intimacy with the Lord: like most college students, I lived like a heathen. In my naïve ignorance, I thought I was a good Christian, because I weekly attended church, participated in a campus Bible Study group, and sang with my church choir and the campus gospel choir. As a more mature Christian, I realize that those are all positive activities, but they don't necessarily reflect a person's closeness to God.

I did, however, pray every day. Prayer was my secret life. I loved to pray. I also recognize that intimate prayer with God can teach one to overcome all kinds of negative circumstances, while training her character to be more like Christ.

Looking back on it now, I know that God's grace and mercy surpasses understanding. With the double life I was living, God had no reason to even hear my prayers or meet me in my time of prayer. He may not have had a logical reason, but God's love always kept the connection open when I approached him with the faith of a child. Today, I better understand what my grandmother meant when she said God takes care of fools and babies: I was both. God always came nearer to me when I sought him.

Those times alone with the Lord kept me grounded during those years when the potential to fall away from him was so great. The Lord gave me courage to live alone off campus. He gave me the wisdom and dedication to stay focused. And he blessed me with wonderful jobs, friends, and family that surrounded me with love and opportunities as a single woman.

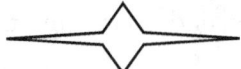

If I hadn't been so broke, my independent college life would have been perfect. Instead, I struggled financially every day of my time at Baylor. Getting by most weeks eating only noodles, potatoes, or beans, I wore the same clothes and shoes year after year. The hardest part of the struggle was my raggedy car. Through God's grace, I was never homeless, hungry, or without necessities.

Those five years of scraping by alone with God definitely gave me the strength to rise above the opinions of other people; even my friends made jokes about me. My friends laughed because they thought I drove my ugly car around with the attitude that it was a BMW or something classy. I never got mad at them, because they were right. In the wintertime, the car's heat was so limited that I kept a brick that I had warmed in the stove on the floorboard to keep my feet warm. Because the car was always breaking down, I kept forty dollars in my ashtray to pay for the inevitable tow truck.

Despite their criticisms of my car, I was blessed with great friends and family. Without solicitation, they bought me clothes, gas, food, and even paid a bill or two. So it never upset me when they laughed at my car. Besides, I knew most of them didn't understand that I was not living in the present. I had my mind set on my dream. In my dreams, I always had more than enough of everything.

Most of my friends and Herb, were living on their parents' financial support, so it was easy for me to make light of their

Learning to Pray Together

opinions. How could they understand my struggle? I wasn't even sure if Herb, as my future husband, would be able to comprehend how much I had sacrificed to remain at Baylor.

So, I prayed about that, too.

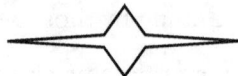

On one hand, I really believed that God was answering my prayer for my future after college, while also speaking to my desire for real love. I just still wondered if Herb was truly God's answer for my lifelong partner.

Long after our engagement, I continued to doubt if I should be planning to marry. It gave me joy to imagine being married to Herb with a family, but I became equally overjoyed at the thoughts of freedom and riches. I remember the night Herb asked me what I wanted out of life.

I quickly answered, "Fame and riches!"

I'll never forget the disappointment that came over his face.

Herb and I were such a great complement to each other, even as young as we were. Where I was independent, he was dependent. Where I was loud and reactive, he was a quiet gentleman. There were even times that I was intimidated by his intelligence that he'd gleaned from reading all of those books. I am an extrovert, and he's an introvert.

When I confessed that I wanted fame and riches, Herb was terrified. All he truly wanted was a family and stability. We should have talked about this more, but we were too in love to care. Looking back, it was such a mistake not to have talked more openly about our divergent hopes and dreams.

It took me a long time to begin to appreciate Herb's "family man" personality. He was the type of mature man who didn't allow himself to be seen in the company of just any person, because he had a family man's reputation to protect. His image had to honor his parents. I eventually came to admire Herb's recognition of serving as a beacon for our family and protecting our image, but at the time it sometimes felt uncomfortable that someone would consider honoring other people so intentionally; this was definitely *not* anything I had seen from most of the adults in my life.

Herb was also slow moving, because he so enjoyed observing the world; I wasn't like that. I was always too busy to smell the flowers. I was also too busy working and trying to survive on my own, while Herb lived in the dorm room paid for by his parents. Because Herb wasn't working at any jobs, and really didn't have anything pressing to do, he used that time to improve himself intellectually and to fall in love with life. Even in the early days of our friendship, I learned to appreciate Herb's views of the world. I might not have been ready to participate in all of that slow-moving reflection and life experience, but I was learning to value it in him.

Learning to Pray Together

Herb was my fiancé, but he sure felt more like a best friend. I would have been content to stay as best friends for much longer, but Herb was persistent in his desire to marry me very soon. For some reason, I never asked Herb why he was so motivated to marry so quickly. I knew I would have married Herb someday, if I could overcome my anxiety about paying for and finishing college.

I was afraid, however, that Herb's immaturity and lack of experience with the realities of bills and lean times might not prepare him to suffer with me through the life I had experienced until then. His answer to my concerns was that we were both poor. Herb didn't seem to understand that his version of poor came with a financial safety net from his parents, while my poorness had no backup plan. We were not yet living on the same plane of life.

After meeting Herb's family for the first time, I saw how committed he was to them and I fell even deeper in love with him. He had a family that I had only dreamed of as a kid while I watched "The Cosby Show." On the outside looking in, his family life was perfect! Another layer of fear left me.

For a time, I had a great relationship with Herb's family. Things changed rapidly, however, after Herb announced our engagement to them. Being rational and strong-willed parents wanting the best for their young son, Herb's parents refused to bless our future marriage. In fact, Herb's parents insisted that we cancel the engagement and break up entirely.

Words cannot express how devastating their actions were to our young joy and our hopeful potential. Herb and I were thrown completely off balance. While I might have been hesitant about how quickly I would be ready to marry him, I was overwhelmed by the prejudice and intensity of my future in-laws' reactions. Obviously, their Cosby-family aura did not run very deep. What had God been thinking, I wondered?

Today, Herb and I are the parents of two teenagers who we adore more than life itself. With this understanding, we can better appreciate Herb's parents' hesitation to bless our proposed union. We were, after all, barely twenty years old. Honestly, I cannot imagine my children marrying at such an early age. At that time, however, Herb and I were devastated by their reaction. I had grown fond of them and believed that they had grown fond of me. I had spent weekends at their home, gone on family trips, and been given a spot in the family...or so I thought. I was so disappointed.

Unfortunately, after Herb announced his plans to marry me, his parents gave him an ultimatum...it was either them or me, but he couldn't have both.

On the other hand, my family adored Herb. Many people were surprised that I desired to marry Herb, or any man for that matter. Herb was a most shocking choice to my closest confidants;

however, because he was so different from anyone I had ever allowed to come around my family. But my family loved Herb because they could see what I saw in him: Herb was such a good man.

Having my family's support meant the world to me, because Herb refused to call off our engagement. Though he had always been dependent to his family's finances and preferences, he chose me over them. Herb lost his entire world, but gained me. At times, I still wonder what we were thinking!

Life with Herb became chaotic after we refused to call off our engagement. My future in-laws did many desperate things over the next several months in their attempt to convince Herb to not marry me. In hindsight, because the Bible says we wrestle not against flesh and blood, I believe that it was the enemy that was manipulating all of Herb's parents' fears so that they did many foolish things.

But God always has a back-up plan!

After a myriad of failed elopements, a crashed wedding, and a two-week breakup after the publicly humiliating non-wedding, Herb and I were finally married nine months after we fell in love. By the grace of God, we overcame much pressure, heartache, and strain. Perhaps in the future I should write a book entitled, "How Not to Elope!"

Herb and I married in a private ceremony that was performed by the same minister who had led us through a "boot camp"-style marriage counseling course just a week before the wedding. We even continued with another week of Christian marriage counseling after the wedding. Today, Herb and I are still reaping the benefits of these sessions. Thank God for wisdom!

Only seven months after our wedding, our daughter, Jade, was born. Two weeks later, I graduated from college. Six months after my graduation, Herb graduated. Life was moving very fast! Two years and eight months into our marriage, Herb and I became parents to our son, Trey. Glory to God!

Because Herb and I met as students, studying together was a normal activity for our lives together. After marriage, we began reading all sorts of books on marriage, communication, and God's purpose for our lives. When we had studied during our early courtship we had been excited and thrilled over the possibilities our new life together. In contrast, during our early marriage, we were shell-shocked from the battles we had waged just trying to marry, and it was a difficult time to find our equilibrium—even with the wisdom of the books on relationships.

Realize that Herb had hurt me deeply. In an attempt to compromise with his parents, he had abandoned me and called off our wedding just four days before the ceremony. I hadn't thought we could recover as a couple from the backlash of those powerful emotions. But, two weeks later, we eloped.

Unfortunately, in response to our elopement, Herb's parents completely disowned him. While I was still reeling from the roller coaster of emotions of his abandonment and subsequent passion to marry me despite the consequences, Herb also struggled with intense emotions. His parents' rejection left Herb devastated and emotionally distant from me for months. It was not as if we were enjoying a romantic honeymoon by anyone's definition!

And, despite my own strengths to overcome the adversities of my life to that point, I felt helpless and angered over the situations. Not even the self-help books seemed to have a tangible answer for me, as I waited on the sidelines as Herb slowly overcame the shock of his seemingly Cosby-like family's uncharacteristic behaviors. Even though Herb did return to himself, the bitterness and resentment he experienced against his parents took years for the Lord to heal in his broken heart. Again, not an ideal situation in which to start life as a young couple.

My own fears and insecurities about relationships, commitments, and families flooded my thoughts and emotions. Had I really given up my seemingly safe independence to jump head-long into the deep anger from being abandoned by my fiancé a few days before our wedding to then battle the guilty feelings of the dissolution of Herb's family? I was reminded of the helplessness my brother and I felt when our parents would argue so intensely at night. And, yet, I felt even more alone in my new married life as family structures and deep fears manifested themselves in such dysfunctional ways.

From my perspective, I believed that Herb possessed the world in his family: they had seemed so much more stable and grounded than my family's behaviors. So, I questioned why Herb believed I was so valuable to him and worth losing his fortress to be with me, instead of staying connected to them. Weren't their riches what I had imagined would give my life purpose and stability?

Why couldn't Herb and I have each other and stay connected with our families? I wished we could have had both. Despite all of the emotional and financial hurdles my seemingly simpler family had overcome, I could not imagine being cut off by them. My mama and my brother had been my life and they had graciously given me over to Herb. As my family stood faithfully in my corner in the event that I needed their support during the trials of my young marriage, Herb's corner was suddenly void of a life's worth of support. The contrast was not only painfully ironic to me; it fueled my insecurities about Herb's logic and our ability to overcome these challenges as a young couple.

Not only was I incapable of understanding the death he must have experienced in his heart, I was terrified that he hadn't truly realized who I was or that I didn't deserve that high a price. I doubted that Herb could truly commit to a lifetime of being my husband if he couldn't also remain the favored son of his own parents.

Coupled with the responsibility of being the "chosen one" were also my continued fears about our lives together. We were

Learning to Pray Together

broke! We went from living separately as poor singles to being married and spending every day and night together as a poor couple. And, then, in an effort to overcompensate for the guilt I felt of Herb losing his family ties and to mask my own fears about the lack of money, I sought to fill his life with activities. As Business students, we scheduled all of our final classes so that we could share everything together. And, in my naiveté, I rationalized that at least we weren't fighting about money, since we didn't have any.

In hindsight, I was grappling to stay in control of succeeding at my dreams of graduation so that I could become that queen of freedom and riches. I was too immature to properly process the whirlwind of emotions and poor choices we were experiencing, so I stuffed my fears and doubts and occupied myself as the organizational leader when my young husband was incapable of leading us through those fiery trials. Today, in an odd way, I am thankful that Herb and I battled together through those challenges, but I would never wish such a difficult set of circumstances on any other couple!

A few months before Herb and I eloped, we discovered that I was pregnant. Obviously, despite the devastating effects of my previous affair, I had not yet learned that there are reasons why God advocates that sex be limited within the confines of marriage. Personally, the pregnancy seemed like a devastating blow to my desire for control and my plans to travel the world as the queen.

Additionally, because we were knee-deep in an emotional war with Herb's parents, Herb addressed the pregnancy news as quietly and calmly as I have learned he always does when he is overwhelmed with unexpected challenges. That bookworm nature of my more introverted husband was almost too present for me to handle at the surprise that we were to have a baby at our young, poor ages.

In addition, I was angry and jealous that it seemed that Herb's dreams of having a family were coming to pass while my life was spiraling out of control. On top of those already complex emotions, I immediately started having nightmares that Herb would abandon the baby and me like my irresponsible dad had abandoned my mama, my brother, and me. I was filled with anxiety day and night.

As if the turmoil of the previous months wasn't enough, our young marriage took an even bigger turn for the worse when my body struggled with the pregnancy. Not only did I endure horrible morning sickness on top of the complexities of Herb's parents' disownment of us, but also the money problems I had tried to ignore became the primary topic of discussion. We needed money for my medical needs, more food, and graduation stuff. Marriage, pregnancy, graduation, and life require funding, and we were still broke!

Unexpectedly, Herb's leadership skills arose as he insisted that I quit work and focus on graduating. Not only did he understand the necessity of completing that goal and preparing us

Learning to Pray Together

for our future together, but Herb recognized that my body needed to rest for the sake of our child. And, surprisingly, I trusted Herb's counsel and quit my job.

Those last few months of school and pregnancy solidified the partnership that Herb and I had forged during our courtship. Buried in books and demonstrating academic success—despite the naysayers who criticized our choices—we both rose to the occasion. Failure was never part of our plan and we did have a plan. Herb overcame his privileged upbringing and went to work after school. We even took a few night classes together to make sure that we'd graduate sooner rather than later. Despite the busyness of work, school, and pregnancy, Herb and I both excelled in our grades that last semester. These aspects of our life, as complex as they were, seemed easy. Our married relationship itself, however, was nearly overwhelming!

Our marriage was hard work. On one hand, fighting for survival thrust us together closer than we ever thought we could be. We were determined not to fail at school and life even if it was just to prove all of our critics wrong. Because we had both been academically successful as singles, it was somehow comfortable to bury ourselves into the books and papers instead of more directly processing and healing from the emotional wounds of the abandoned wedding and being cut off from Herb's family.

Dying to Become One

On the other hand, we felt so alone and lost. When we had been hopefully planning our married life together, our vision had nothing to do with being abandoned by Herb's parents, being pregnant so quickly, or shifting our working responsibilities as quickly as my health had required. The tornado of change and emotional upheaval was breath taking. At times, we wondered if we could survive another day with the devastating loss of Herb's family from our lives.

When a family is torn apart unexpectedly, it is truly a kind of death. There is a deep hole that is torn into the hearts of everyone involved. Oh, of course, strong willed people like Herb, his parents, and me are capable of masking the loss and stumbling through the day with some semblance of acceptability, but the wound is real. In an odd way, if the loss is caused by an unexpected physical death, then those left behind are allowed to grieve while friends and family rush in to support the emotional transition of life. With the emotional death of abandonment, however, the wounded parties do not receive all of that support to better transition to life without their loved ones: friends just find the whole situation awkward, so the wounded heart just festers in isolation.

Even though my family loved and supported us, they couldn't replace what was lost. And none of us could remove the dark cloud that dwelled with Herb as he, understandably, struggled

Learning to Pray Together

in silence of this unexpected death. Herb had envisioned a lifetime of family weekends with his parents and sisters to share the joy of his wonderful bride. Instead, unexpectedly, Herb was shunned from sharing his joy and detached from the grounded wisdom of a lifetime. Herb's life was not what he had envisioned when he asked me to marry him.

We were so alone.

While Herb suffered in private and grieved over the removal of his emotional safety net of his family, I felt like I was suffering the public death of my identity as a proud and successful woman. Remember, I had fallen in love with Herb after the difficult affair I had hidden from the bright lights of the Christian campus at Baylor. While Herb had been thrilled to share with the entire campus that we were a couple, I had been hesitant to shift my public identity that quickly. Yes, I loved Herb, but couldn't we just keep it a bit quieter?

Instead, it was as if God allowed a huge spotlight to shine on us as we shared our whirlwind romance with our two, large, circles of campus friends. And the lights felt even brighter as we planned an elaborate wedding that was subsequently shattered by Herb's parents. Not only did I have to deal with the rejection of Herb's parents towards me, and then Herb's own rejection of me for a short time, but I felt humiliated at being left "at the altar" in front of my entire social network!

On top of these devastations, my early and difficult pregnancy then became new fodder for the Christian campus' gossip circles, or at least that was part of my imagined embarrassment as my growing belly made it physically and socially uncomfortable for me to even attend class. At that stage of my life, I still held onto my pride and ego like a protective cloak. So, I struggled with my sense of self as I waddled around campus looking like a beach ball, when for the past five years I had literally ruled and reigned at Baylor. The emotional, hormonal, and social pressures were just too much for me!

After about three months of marriage, the pressure of marriage, school, pregnancy, and the unresolved emotions of the chaos of our union finally bubbled over in screaming matches at home. Herb and I had never fought before we married. We had disagreed, but we had always talked our differences through as rational, logical people. This was different. This was frustration, un-forgiveness, fear, harbored anger, his parents' rejection, and hard times yelling through our immature and inexperienced selves who had endured so much hardship in such a short amount of time.

Herb and I would yell and then ignore each other afterwards. Because the anger was so intense and undirected, we might argue and then forget why we were even mad in the first place. Looking back, I begin to recognize that these tantrums were similar to the fights that my brother and I observed when my mama and step-dad started fighting. Unfortunately, unresolved

Learning to Pray Together

hurts and the frustrations of life can bubble up in anger in any generation that is not trained to acknowledge and process these issues with love and maturity. And, without new counsel, grown children often resort to the same dysfunctional behaviors that they have observed in their childhood homes.

Had I become my mama?

Herb's previous life of leisure was completely disrupted at this point in our marriage, and we were both frustrated by it. All through college, Herb had happily adapted to a comfortable routine: classes in the morning, cafeteria-prepared meals when he wanted, an afternoon nap, and evening studies at the library. That quiet, routine life was over, and Herb struggled with a rigorous class schedule, jobs he hated, ungodly study hours just to keep up, and a sick and cranky wife with whom he had to learn to share meal preparation responsibilities.

Obviously, Herb was frazzled from all of the emotional and practical changes of his life, but I grew even more angry and resentful with how he sought to find balance amongst all of his chaos. I was clueless as to how or why he could expend effort quitting and seeking multiple jobs, just because he realized that each job was not to his liking. How dare he demonstrate inconsistency and apparent selfishness while I was already struggling with relinquishing control of my independence, my finances, my body's changes, and my future in front of the entire university student body?!

It was all much more than I could take.

Desperate to escape from the hell of living in total strife with my husband of a few months, I called my Aunt Irene who had been married to my Uncle Thelbert all of my life. They were also pastors, so I wondered if or how they might help me overcome the frustration of arguing continually with my husband but never coming to a resolution. There had to be a way off of the merry-go-round of torment.

Aunt Irene and Uncle Thelbert were priceless jewels in my life. Not only were they strong Christian towers in the community, but also they had been wise counselors to my mama through many challenging phases of her life.

Even in my childhood memories, Aunt Irene and Uncle Thelbert's home was as important to me as that of my mama and my grandmother. I attended the same church with my Aunt and Uncle for several years, often enjoying their company, as they would return me home after mama had placed my brother and me on the church bus each week. Their wisdom and comfort were valuable to me as I struggled to deal with mama's fighting or other unwise choices when I was a child.

Frankly, Aunt Irene and Uncle Thelbert's home was always a stabilizing environment of love and encouragement, even during my college years, when I might visit with them more frequently than my own mama. I remember Aunt Irene's home as the largest

Learning to Pray Together

one I ever visited as a child, and I marveled at its fancy décor and peaceful, godly family environment: such a contrast from my mama's home.

Despite being so glamorous, Aunt Irene was always there for me. She was especially available when I needed to learn about how to have a wonderful marriage. Obviously, Herb and I were not yet skilled in that area of our lives.

Aunt Irene and Uncle Thelbert's wisdom emanated from their understanding of love. I had always known they loved me, and I was grateful for how much they loved Herb. More importantly, however, they loved the union of God's holy matrimony and they treated it as sacred. Believing the Bible's teaching that marriage is a covenant between a man and a woman and the Lord, these human pastors taught that marriage should be handled with care. In that loving environment, I knew I could trust the wise and godly counsel I would receive from Aunt Irene about how best grow my chaotic family to be more like hers.

As I poured out my angry and frightened tears for more than thirty minutes to glamorous Aunt Irene, I heard only one word of counsel couched in a soft bit of laughter, "Pray."

"What?!" my inner thoughts wanted to rage. I, obviously, wasn't laughing. "What does that even mean?!" I wanted to shout.

In her gracious manner, Aunt Irene continued. "Pray, Nisha. You commit to praying by yourself each day, and then you and Herb pray together every day."

"But, Aunt Irene, Herb is such a private introvert. I don't think he'll be willing to pray out loud with me. Yeah, he prays alone about important things, but he wouldn't know what to do with me next to him."

"Okay. Then start with where you are. Be real, but start simply. You don't have to pray complex prayers like you do in private, Nisha. Even if he just sits there quietly, ask him to join you daily for a time of prayer. Trust me, over time, he'll build up his courage. Ya'll are "one" now, Nisha, and you need to be "one" that prays together.

"Oh, and you need to read the Bible together each day."

What kind of advice was that from Aunt Irene? I was so disappointed and discouraged! Didn't she realize I needed to know how to motivate Herb to be more outgoing and to keep a steady job? Didn't she realize I needed Herb to take more responsibility so I might one day regain my independence? What was Aunt Irene thinking?!

And, yet, deep down, I knew that her wisdom had never previously failed me. She had been happily married for thirty years and I had yet to feel successful in marriage for more than thirty minutes at a time. Her life and her stories motivated me that even

Learning to Pray Together

Herb and I could learn to fight alongside each other through the rough seasons of life, rather than continue to fight each other. I at least had enough sense and humility to figure out how to apply Aunt Irene's counsel before considering a different option.

Thankfully, despite my insecurities about inviting Herb, he willingly agreed to participate in daily Bible studies and prayer. Of course, Herb didn't volunteer to start praying out loud, but he was present. I'll never forget our first prayer time. I prayed, "Lord, we gave you our marriage, please help us, in the name of Jesus. Amen." That was it.

I don't remember the scripture we read that first day, but I'll never forget that first prayer. I was so excited that Herb and I were praying together. Prayer had always been my secret life that I had rarely shared with anyone besides my childhood friend Peter, but now I was sharing prayer with the love of my life.

So began our devotional time together. Herb and I met daily to pray and read a scripture. It was simple: I read a scripture and then prayed. We didn't discuss the scripture at first, but slowly Herb and I began to talk about it. Some days, especially if we were fighting because of the challenges of our young, crazy lives, I would just pray, "God, please help us. Amen."

After a few weeks of simple prayers and devotions, Herb volunteered to pray. I screamed with joy on the inside, but I kept my cool and found and read the scripture. Progress! It was a miracle. The Lord had opened the door for us to grow together in him and it was working. We started out praying for our marriage, our family, our finances, and for Jade, our unborn child. Over time, we also began to pray for others, the world, and the less fortunate than us.

All of these years later, Herb and I still pray and study together. We have also trained our children so that we pray as a family now, study God's word as a family, and share our lives lived in and through Christ as a family. Daily we come together as a family to celebrate the blessings of God, to gain refreshment from his word, and to be quick to share any hurts or transgressions we have experienced. Within this format, our family is diligent to repent and forgive quickly, while trusting God's ways for every area of our lives.

Glory to God! For he has grown our prayers, deepened our Bible studies, strengthened our marriage, and multiplied our family. Despite the isolation of the nearly overwhelming trials of our early-married life, Herb and I are thankful that we learned in those seasons to lean on each other, to develop our own family's practices and traditions, and to trust that God and his ways are the best.

God bless Aunt Irene for having the spirit of wisdom to give the kind of advice that brings life, heals, and restores!

Learning to pray together

I am so passionate about couples praying together that I encourage you to determine how and when to begin praying with your spouse. Start simply as Herb and I did. Remember, the two of you are learning to be "one," so take Aunt Irene's wise counsel and start praying together. And as you grow in confidence with praying and speaking aloud with the person you love and trust the most, allow God's word to continue to change you from the inside out.

Overcoming with Prayer

So prayer became the new weapon of choice as Herb and I learned to overcome things that tried to destroy our marriage. We prayed about everything, including the deep hurts caused by Herb's parents' rejection. Over time, we learned a lot more about prayer in the process. The first thing Herb and I learned is that God answers prayers.

Seriously, I am here to tell you that God answers prayer. You probably know people who don't really believe that God has the time or the desire to answer prayers. But that is incorrect. Frankly, God jumps at the chance to answer the prayers of people who have actually humbled themselves and prayed to him.

Think about it: in order to pray you must first believe that God's listening and that he's real. That's called faith and God loves faith.

Next, you are actually humbling yourself to ask the God of the universe for help. Wow! And God realizes how much courage that takes for you to get out of your own way and ask him for help. Realize that humility brings much grace from God.

Finally, you have to believe that God will deliver what you pray for, another act of faith in him and his character. Trusting him gets easier once you are consistent in praying and receiving his answers.

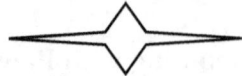

As Herb and I were learning to pray, we began to pray about everything important to a couple: sex, parents, the kids, money, what trips to take, what jobs to look at...everything. It was like the more we prayed, the faster God answered the prayers.

Beyond the answers to specific prayers, we were also thrilled with the "side benefits." As Herb and I began to pray for each other in each other's presence, it became harder to fight. As we transparently sought our heavenly father's perspective about our personal issues, we exposed our earnest desires and our deepest fears to one another. We were learning to trust one another as much as we were learning to trust God.

Through my many tears as I asked God to prepare me to be a good mother after his heart, Herb came to understand how terrified I was of motherhood. Not only would being a mother challenge my independent plans, but my childhood fears and disappointments were harping at my desire to always be in control and to not fail at such a large responsibility. Herb also learned through my prayers that, despite my get-to-it attitude at home, I truly had a desire to be a good wife even though I had very little experience about what that would look like.

Similarly, Herb became more verbal in our private times with God, and I learned how to pray for him more effectively.

Rather than continuing to desire that Herb become more like me, I grew to pray that he would become more like God designed him.

I marveled at the results we experienced as our prayers were answered so clearly, especially when we practiced personalizing God's scriptures for our prayers, instead of just making up words to fit our mind's image of what we desired. God's words and his ways really do work! And God demonstrated how much he loved our marriage and us with each answered prayer.

One of the amazing results of our prayers was related to Herb's parents. Remember, we had begun to pray for peace and reconciliation with them once we learned to pray together. Just before Jade's birth, my in-laws decided that they wanted to be a part of their grandchild's life, despite their previous ultimatum to disown Herb if he married me.

While we knew in our hearts that there would be long-term benefits for our families to have my in-laws re-engaged with Herb and our family, we were also fearful and stressed about how the first meeting would transpire. I was especially uncomfortable about seeing them again because I had gained over sixty pounds with the pregnancy: my self-esteem was even lower than it had been with the emotional upheavals of canceled wedding plans and parental abandonment. Frankly, I wasn't excited about reuniting while looking a "hot mess."

Of course, Herb was thankful about the reconciliation, but he still worried if we could actually all get along peacefully as he had previously envisioned. He had ample reason to worry: not only had he been living with a cranky pregnant wife, but he had also learned how volatile I could become when I was angry. While neither Herb or I were yet very experienced with emotional healing, Herb was wise enough to recognize that I was still very hurt and angry because of his parents' actions: they had rejected us as a couple, ruined my wedding, and wounded the man I loved. Herb was beginning to realize that I have the ability to defend my own like a mother bear protects her cubs when I believe we are being threatened. That image must have kept Herb up at night, imagining what that could look like through the always-socially-correct aura of his childhood family's eyes.

Despite my growing experiences that God answers prayer, Herb and I prayed to God about the visit, traveled to my in-laws' home, and experienced a visit as horrible and uncomfortable as I had imagined it would be. We four adults pretended to be polite, ignoring the difficult topics of the last six months that had upended all of our lives.

I tried to hide my fat, pregnant self from the judgmental eyes of my in-laws, as they continued to belittle my self-worth and me. Neither side had yet recognized the jealousy and control we had for wanting Herb in our lives on our own terms, nor had we considered how to maturely address or integrate our different upbringings and desired futures for one another.

I was so grateful when Herb and I were finally free to leave his parents' home that visit. I was tired of stuffing my anger and pretending to be polite and respectful despite all of the guilt and shame I felt I had experienced because of their immature yet controlling influences on my life; how dare they try to rein me in! Didn't they know I was to be a queen to rule the world?!

As if I needed more salt in my emotional wounds, Herb mentioned on the drive home that his dad had wondered aloud if I would ever lose all of the baby weight. Really?! Not only did this insult reinforce my own low self-esteem, it was especially hurtful because it had come from the man whom I had originally thought was as wise and kind as Bill Cosby's television role. How is it that when we have an emotional weakness because of bad childhood circumstances that the enemy can seem capable to magnify our fears in the places where we would hope to feel the safest?

Herb and I visited with his parents with mixed results a few more times before Jade's due date. It was still difficult for all of us to tiptoe around the un-discussed issues, but we kept trying. The real start to reconciliation actually took place in the hospital birthing room.

Different than the visits in my in-laws' home, the four of us were joined at the hospital by my mama and the handful of doctors and nurses as I delivered Jade. My body that had been so

Overcoming with Prayer

challenged during the pregnancy didn't make Jade's delivery any easier. I was in labor for thirty hours! I have always believed that it was Jade's objective to force all of her family to spend time together.

There is something significant about witnessing the miracle and pain of a God-given birth with other people. In the moment, it didn't feel that meaningful for me, because all I felt was pain for a day and a night with no sleep. In hindsight, however, I remember the mothers laughing, crying, and worrying together. I began to see similarities of motherhood between my mama, my mother-in-law, and even myself. A spark of hope for a peaceful family life was truly birthed in my own heart that day.

Herb and I were so proud, because we were the parents of the first grandchild for both of our families. And our families acknowledged their love for us and the child that God had birthed between our families, even if those specific words were not necessarily spoken on that day.

Even our friends were proud of us. Over thirty friends came and stayed at the hospital for the entire ordeal. Even though I had struggled with the shame of other people's opinions as I had driven my raggedy car, worn the same clothes every year, hid my unfortunate affair, felt off-balanced with a whirlwind campus romance, and then lived through the embarrassment of both my failed wedding and my uncomfortable pregnancy weight gain, I felt so loved and accepted that day in the hospital!

It's one of the most beautiful moments of my life.

Dying to Become One

Only two weeks after Jade was born, I graduated from Baylor. My maturing dreams were coming true and God was answering our prayers. My beautiful daughter was healthy and happy, and I was beginning to learn how to be a good mother. Herb was on track to graduate the following semester, and I was demonstrating how I could be a loving wife. While Herb continued to work and go to school, I also worked as a substitute teacher, fulfilling both my interests to be useful outside the home and to improve our financial situation.

And Herb's parents were more involved with us more than ever. My mother-in-law frequently babysat Jade while we worked. We were so grateful for their growing support of our young family.

By the grace of God, it seemed that Herb and I had overcome the impossible! All the glory definitely goes to the Lord for that family foundation that has become so firm over the decades. It might have been a rough, hard beginning, but it was a united beginning, all the same.

As Herb's graduation date drew near, Herb and I were praying consistently to ask the Lord to direct us to where he would have us to go. We believed we should look for employment in a larger city. Continuing to be transparent before one another in our daily prayer time, however, I learned that Herb was nervous about maybe living in a large city and that he was uncertain if he would secure a good job. Because of my growing trust in Herb, however,

Overcoming with Prayer

I believed in him like never before. I was confident that any company would be blessed to have him!

"The sky's the limit!" was my daily confession, still dreaming of how I could one day rule the world.

My unwavering faith and beliefs for God's greatness to materialize in our married lives still seemed crazy to the logical introvert I had for a husband. But after graduating against all odds, my faith in the impossible had gone through the roof.

Just as the young shepherd David remembered how he had killed the lion and the bear as he stood in front of the giant Goliath, I remembered how far God's grace had brought me in the last five years. I thought of the girl who had been dropped off at Baylor University by herself, despite the limited income and social challenges of a dysfunctional family. I thought of how she dared to believe that she could be the first in her family to earn a college degree from Baylor University, if she didn't quit or allow herself to be distracted. I was encouraged and full of faith by all that I—through God's grace—had done, especially realizing with how little I had started.

The daily prayer times with Herb and me eventually focused on our different perspectives on God. Like our earlier prayer topics, we didn't understand the value of being more equally yoked with one another about God until our differences became another source of frustration in our marriage.

On one hand, I constantly encouraged myself by thinking on all that Herb and I had already accomplished by faith. I trusted that God was going to bless us mightily and we wouldn't have any worries. On the other hand, Herb's practical and slow-moving personality wanted to understand every step of the upcoming changes before he was comfortable to modify his daily routine. Eventually, I became impatient with Herb's doubts, as if they were the reason I wasn't yet living my dreams more fully. Similarly, Herb became frustrated with my illogical and foolish go-for-it zeal.

Leaning on the wise counsel of Aunt Irene, Herb and I just took these differences to the Lord in prayer. I asked God to increase Herb's faith, while my husband asked God to give me more patience.

Today, Herb and I know that it was our decision to pray together and follow God's leading that made us victorious in those early years. The same practices of trusting God and being transparent before one another has sustained us through many more seasons of trials and tribulations.

It has been in our prayer times that our merciful, heavenly father has given us keys to overcoming everything that tries to stand in the way of his best for our lives. Pride, foolishness, fleshly desires, sickness, poverty, depression, etc., cannot stay around our lives for long when we consistently and humbly seek God's ways of doing everything in our married lives.

Overcoming with Prayer

We bless His holy name, for He is good!

Overcoming in prayer

As you and your spouse continue to spend time together daily in the Bible and in prayer, what issues concern you most? Do they include family, children, money, jobs, or God's will for your lives as Herb and I experienced? Whatever the challenges, keep your commitment to stay united with one another and with God. I promise that learning to overcome the challenges of life using God's way truly is the best thing possible!

Discovering Who You are as "One"

Our marriage was an infant. Herb and I didn't believe that we had any advice to offer anyone, but the Lord had other plans. Even before we had been married a year, other couples started asking us for our advice, just as I had done with my Aunt Irene.

Feeling inadequate and unqualified to give advice, Herb and I often referred young couples to the same books that we had read. We hoped those experienced authors would guide the couples into more wisdom while we struggled to work through our own issues. But the couples returned seeking *our* advice, despite our attempts to push them away time and time again. We were confused as to why other people wanted to hear about our experiences.

Mostly, I was asked, "How do ya'll do this?" Or, "Why is your marriage so solid?"

Many couples said they wanted the close friendship that Herb and I shared. They wanted to know—despite all the negativity that Herb and I had endured publicly and financially—how had we achieved the comfort with each other that is usually reserved for a couple who has been together over thirty years.

With our little knowledge of the Word of God and only a few challenging months of marriage, Herb and I had stumbled onto something that others believed they needed. We did not understand it, but we have since learned that God's ways are higher than our own. Even when Herb and I felt unqualified, the Lord confirmed time and again that He had put the two of us together to become "one" for a specific purpose: to bless other married couples.

Now a rational person would not declare "Victory!" over a few months of marriage, but our few months of marriage were unlike most. We had overcome many hurdles in our short time together. Even with that in mind, we were still among the rational thinkers and thought the idea of helping others with marriage advice was simply ridiculous.

But, more importantly, we had dug deeper and deeper into the Word of God. And, with Him, we were learning that when the Lord creates something, he has a purpose for that thing. A marriage is no different: the union of two people does not allow two individuals to live side by side. Instead, a marriage is a new creation where the two people are to become "one." For whatever the reason, then, the Lord was using our marriage as a sign or a witness to help other young couples. Long before we knew *how* to help them, we were called by God to help married couples learn how to grow into being "one" with each other.

Godly people with supernatural vision have confirmed our God-given destiny time and time again. They say that my husband and I look like "family" to them. Other observers see a big red bow tied around us. Thus, despite our limited spiritual vision for our God-given assignment, the Lord was blessing Herb and me with something that other people could sense and they desired to learn from us. The magnitude of this supernatural assignment from the Lord—as crazy as it felt—was confirmed to us even beyond the observations of other people. I even began to have my own visions about our responsibility to assist young couples.

In one of my visions, I saw crowds of people in our front yard just hanging out. When I went out onto my front porch to inspect the situation, everyone rushed up to me. Behind them, through the break in the crowds, I saw a row of washers and dryers.

Overwhelmed, I started asking the people to get off our property and to take their washers and dryers with them. As the people started leaving, they paired up in couples, as I then assumed they had arrived. But they were leaving empty-handed.

I repeated, "Please take your machines with you."

One of the people turned to me and said "Ma'am, those machines were already here. That's why we came here, so we could get washed."

At that point in our walk with God, Herb and I had not yet learned about the anointing of God. The *anointing* is the power of God that enables us to do things we would otherwise be unable to do without him. In the Old Testament, leaders were anointed to do miraculous things, just as the spirit of God rested on the young shepherd David before he brought the giant Goliath down with

Discovering Who You are as "One"

just a slingshot and a stone when the entire army of Israel had been terrified to even face Goliath.

Jesus, the apostles, and believers also had access to God's anointing, as documented in the Book of Acts and throughout Paul's writings to the Church. Holy Spirit represents this New Testament anointing and he manifests in a lot of different ways. In our case, God was anointing us with supernatural counsel, insight, wisdom, and a clearer understanding of families than would be logical based on our upbringings. Sounds crazy, doesn't it?

Just imagine if it were you. How would you feel as young newlyweds floundering to get through many days in peace, and yet other couples kept showing up at your front door asking for help? Well, it was me and Herb. Our insecurities, flaws, and failures all seemed to be visible for the world to see, but the longer we have been married, the more people come seeking help as they desire to be "one" with each other.

Who are you as "one"?

Before I move into addressing the most common questions of newlyweds in the next chapter, take a moment and ask yourselves these questions.

1. What is God's purpose for joining the two of you together as a couple?
2. Do you desire to be "one" with each other?
3. Are you willing to let God's anointing strengthen you as a couple, so that Holy Spirit can help you accomplish tasks that are seemingly impossible without God?

Discovering Who You are as "One"

Learning to Become "One"

To other people it seemed like Herb and I had worked effortlessly through all kinds of problems, but that is so far from the truth. God is big! And his grace and mercy are even bigger! From the very beginning of our marriage, Herb and I learned foundational truths from the Word of God, books, and wise people.

One of the truths we learned is that every marriage—regardless of its age—seeks peace, love, acceptance, and joy. This desire for harmonious victory is at the heart of all marriages. The evident struggle, however, results because so many people do not know how to live in victory. Imagine owning a car that you dreamed about and saved for, only to get it and discover that you do not know how to drive it. What a travesty that would be! I feel that same heartache when I see couples who do not yet know how to live in victory as "one."

In the beginning of sharing about my married life with other young couples, I would just answer their questions by sharing what Herb and I had practiced. We were beginning to see positive results from what we were doing and we intentionally sought to apply only the techniques that were in alignment with God's Word.

Today, I still advocate that anyone who is teaching or advising someone else should only preach what you already practice.

Now, after almost two decades of marriage and living transparently before other couples, very rarely do I ever believe that a marriage is beyond help. And, in those rare situations, it is usually when a spouse has begun abusing the other person, verbally, mentally, or physically. And those situations require specific and trained counsel that I will not address in this book.

Thus, even though Herb and I have learned more about the deeper complexities of each unique relationship, the importance of addressing cultural and background differences of each spouse, and the necessity of being equally joined to one another, there are still some basic topics I can address for you. In my experience, most first-time newlyweds ask the same questions:

1. How do we stop fighting? Why are we getting on each other's nerves when we were so crazy in love with each other?
2. Why does my spouse allow his/her parents, friends, or family in our business?
3. Should we share our bank accounts, money, and belongings?

Each of these questions is important enough, that I will focus each of the next three chapters on only one topic at a time.

Discovering Who You are as "One"

Are you willing to learn?

If you are as committed to learning to love your marriage as I imagine you are, I encourage you to start planning to address each of these three items as a couple. Here are some suggestions:

1. Start looking ahead to your individual and family schedules. Where and when will you be able to speak about each of the upcoming topics?
2. How will you make the conversation open for real talk without being disturbed? Who will watch the kids? And how long is that person available to help you out?

The point is that there is more work ahead than you may have ever imagined. To learn to love your marriage, you will need to shift priorities and have deep conversations with your spouse. At first it may look impossible, but remember: God and I are rooting you on. But you have to take the first steps to making a change in your marriage. So, start preparing yourselves for change.

Getting Along

The first step of learning to become "one" is to figure out how to stop fighting. The short answer is: stop fighting! But that's usually not much help. Without knowing specifically why you two are fighting, I start with two answers.

First of all, if you are recently married, you have been in the newlywed stage that is comparative to a child with a new toy. Everything has been perfect for a while. Heavenly bliss is another good way to describe it.

However, one day—after joyfully living in heavenly bliss—you come out of the fog and look around and your spouse looks more *normal* to you. Still lovely, but the glow is not as bright. Perhaps this first shift in perception occurs after six months of living together; for other couples, it could be as long a year.

Once the euphoric glow starts to tarnish, you begin to notice little imperfections: he leaves the toilet seat up or she leaves her hair all over the sink. Now these actions are not new; your spouse has always lived like this. But while you were living in the Newlywed Haze, you didn't pay attention to these issues. Now that the "new" is wearing off your vision of your spouse, you are finding out what you really like and what you really do not like.

Despite the seeming frustration, I suggest that this is a good time for you both as you learn to become "one" with each other. It is good because now you have the opportunity to begin discussions that will be the foundation of your life lived together. <u>Confrontation is good; fighting is bad.</u>

People who love each other will have disagreements. In many cases that is how issues are resolved: because you love each other enough to communicate your expectations and learn to work through them together. Unfortunately, in a house where no one ever disagrees, you find secrets and lies. The trick to maturing into a healthy couple is to disagree and then resolve the disagreement without hurting each other.

My husband, Herb, never had an issue with communicating, in general. Instead, he had an issue with my style of communicating, because I was so very direct in the beginning of our marriage. Well, I still am very direct, but I have learned to be more compassionate with my words.

In the beginning of our marriage, Herb wanted to avoid my too direct and "real" truth, so he just refused to share his frustrations about one of my actions until one day…as you may have guessed…he would blow up!! This was never a lovely exchange. We are two very strong, communicative people. And, when we would disagree, it was brutal for both of us.

Once we identified that our arguments were much more about our communication styles instead of what was probably a relatively small difference of preferences, Herb and I chose to behave differently. Despite his fear of my potential reaction or his frustration about our differences, Herb found the courage and the grace to share his disappointments while they were still small. And

I learned that I had to be more sensitive and graceful in my word choices when discussing my husband's observations. Over time, we learned the benefits of discussing a small difference of opinion, rather than creating an environment in which Herb would allow his frustrations to fester and then we would end up in the most confrontational situation I had experienced.

For example, Herb and I respond to social engagements differently. I have always been a social butterfly. I love people, I love company, and I love parties: even now as a die-hard Christian I still party. I don't get drunk or act like a wild heathen, but like Jesus I love to be where people are celebrating. Anyway, like I mentioned before, Herb is the exact opposite. He doesn't mind parties, but he doesn't live for socializing.

In the beginning of our marriage, Herb was perfectly happy to be at home with just the kids and me. But I continued my customary celebrations in my home, having people over all the time. Herb, however, did not socialize at my parties. He might speak to a couple of people, but then he would retreat to his inner thoughts, no matter how many people were around, just like the bookworm that he was when we were first dating.

I was really irritated with Herb's behavior because I envisioned us hosting our parties as a happy couple. Herb, however, had a different vision. He envisioned us alone, enjoying our new life together, away from the crazy, outside world. So, you can see we had a problem. And we saw we had a problem.

Getting Along

I, however, compounded our problem even more when I addressed it the wrong way: "Why don't you socialize? What's wrong with you? You just seem so boring sometimes!"

Now, those are tactless fighting words. Unfortunately, at the time, they were the best words I could find based on my knowledge of marriage, life, and communication techniques. But those words were fight starters, like a spark in dry woods!

Herb's reaction, however, did not erupt into a verbal boxing match. My husband despises confrontation, so he would sit and say nothing. If Herb had a civilized person as a wife, this may have worked; but I was not civilized. The more he avoided the issue, the more I pushed the issue, complete with my hostile form of communication.

After a few days of passively experiencing the festering of his own emotions while I would push his buttons, Herb would snap! He would yell! He would hit the wall. And then Herb would walk out.

I, on the other hand, would sit there confused, trying to figure out when or why he got so mad. I was unable, at first, to recognize how much my behaviors and communication style were fostering his eruptions.

Thankfully, Herb and I could only be this dumb for a short while, because we had committed to praying together every day. Because of our daily prayers, it was obvious that we needed to pray for our arguments, tantrums, and outbursts. Frankly, as we recognized a specific item about our communication problems, we asked God to fix them and he did. Herb learned that avoiding issues never works, and I learned how to speak to him with respect and honor.

Learning to grow together as "one" despite our different communication styles was not easy and it did not happen overnight. But every positive step—especially when God is invited along for the journey—counts. So, I have learned that confrontation with my husband can produce positive results when we each lovingly choose to seek God's wisdom, are willing to learn from our spouse, and are willing to grow into a more mature person by the grace of God.

The second reason newlyweds start fighting or getting on each other's nerves is due to unexpressed expectations. I love how parents in other cultures, like contemporary India, take the young couple through several years of preparation before they get married; unfortunately, in past times Indian women did not have as much freedom as they continue to gain. The families discuss their expectations and the couples express their wants and needs before the marriage and then each person must live up to those expectations. In contrast, Americans typically spend more time and money on the wedding preparations than on the marriage, despite the fact that the marriage lasts much longer than the wedding—even for the shortest of marriages.

The problem with this American approach is that many couples don't discuss practical things before marriage. They assume that all of the practical pieces will fall into place after the wedding.

Wrong! Nothing in this life just falls into place. I even have to comb my hair to make it fall into place, get up and walk to the trash can to make the trash fall into the trash can, or prepare my thoughts and notes to make my meetings fall into place. Most things—I would go so far as to say all things—require some thought or work in order to fall into place. Marriage is no different.

So, if you and your spouse did not discuss practical issues before you got married, then you are overdue for a family meeting. Sit down and give each other the love, respect, and patience you vowed to give to the other person and then talk about the tough issues. OK, who is going to take the trash out and why? Who is going to wash the clothes and why? Why do you want the toilet seat down? Who is going to do the financial planning, or are you both going to work on it daily?

During these conversations, be very honest about your strengths and weaknesses. This is not the time for ego: your home is like a ship, and if the right people are not doing the right things then ship *will* go off course...to "Wherever Land." Before you consider if "Wherever Land" might be fun, let me assure you that "Wherever Land" is NOT cool!

This used to be an issue for Herb and me. My husband assumed that many things were the "man's" job. Unlike Herb who was raised in a traditional two-parent home, I grew up with a single mom for the most part and my view of a "man's" job was a little different. My biological dads lived at several homes in varied relationships, so he didn't take out the trash or do any jobs that fell into my husband's definition of man's work.

Because my home life had been so dysfunctional, I also had a very different view of "woman's" work. My mama worked a lot. Sometimes she would be at work as much as sixty to eighty hours a week, just trying to survive with my brother and me. Because of our dissimilar upbringings, Herb nd I had different expectations about who should be responsible for the boring—but necessary—tasks with running a home.

In addition, I am much more independent and strong-willed than my husband's mother. And, with my passion—and sometimes workaholic—perspective on my life activities outside my home, I did *not* have time for a lot of housework or cooking. I did cook and I did do housework, but I was not happy about it. As a result, Herb and I had some very practical issues to resolve.

I remember talking to a friend, Mrs. D., who was about 73 years old. She was a successful businesswoman, who still went to her boutiques every day. She was very youthful and she and her husband, Mr. Bill, had a great marriage. I shared with Mrs. D., one day, that I was frustrated that Herb wasn't as good as I was with planning our money.

Mrs. D. asked, "Well, is he as good at it as you are?"

"No," I answered, "I earned all A's in accounting class and it comes naturally for me."

Getting Along

"Well, why should Herb manage the money if you're so good at it? Ya'll were put together to complement each other."

Bright lights went off in my head!

Mrs. D. went on to explain that it was this recognition of one another's strengths and weaknesses that was one of the keys to her great marriage to Mr. Bill. They worked to complement each other.

How do you and your spouse complement each other? Are you utilizing your strengths and weaknesses to produce excellence in your goals as a team?

For example, if your spouse is a morning person and you are a night owl, how can you use those differences to bless your home? When our kids were newborns we put those types of differences to work. I took the early morning shifts with the kids and my husband took the late nights. No one was over-worked or frustrated. We each took our turns with the kids in ways that were natural to us.

Once the two of you figure out what your strengths and weaknesses are and how they can complement each other, you need maturity to put into practice the wisdom you've learned. Say, for example, you both discover that one of you loves washing clothes. It may sound strange, yes, but I've seen stranger things. Why should the other person be forced to do laundry if one of you loves doing laundry?

On the other hand, there will be some things neither one of you want to do...like picking up after the dog, washing dishes, doing the yard, or calling the phone company when you know you'll have to be on hold for thirty minutes. These things must be done for the benefit of your family, so you have to discuss, decide, and delegate each task to someone.

Perhaps you take turns with the dirty, hard jobs that no one wants. Or maybe you hire someone else to do those necessary tasks. For years, neither my husband nor I had time to do the yard without sacrificing needed sleep in our very busy lives. As a result of our discussions and decisions, we agreed to budget in the money to hire someone else to mow the lawn. Of course we sacrificed eating meals out during the lean times to allow our limited budget to pay someone else to do the dirty job, but our attention to the practical things keeps our marriage healthy.

The point is: do what you have to do to get along.

Getting Along

Learning to get along

Now it's your turn. Remember how I suggested earlier that you start looking ahead for time to work through deep discussions with your spouse. Here you go! It's time to start making the lists of the necessary tasks, talking about them, and deciding to whom each task is delegated. While each couple is different, I include some thought-starters for you to consider.

Get creative. Talk about your strengths and weaknesses, your expectations and preferences. And be honest! If you hate cleaning the toilet, then say so. At the same time, realize that *someone* has to clean the toilet.

Dying to Become One

Do what you have to do to get along

Necessary Task	Who's better at it?	Who's weaker at it?	Delegate to:	When? Under what conditions
Dinner Dishes	Husband Wife Both Neither	Husband Wife Both Neither	Husband Wife Both Someone Else	**H:** *M,T,Th* **W:** *W,Sat* *Eat out Fri/Sun by saving on groceries with coupons*
Grocery Shopping	Husband Wife Both Neither	Husband Wife Both Neither	Husband Wife Both Someone Else	**W:** *Make a list by Sun pm* **H:** *Find coupons by Sun pm* **Both:** *H shop at bargain store and W shop at specialty stores by Tue eve*
Financial Planning & Budgeting	Husband Wife Both Neither	Husband Wife Both Neither	Husband Wife Both Someone Else	
Pay Bills	Husband Wife Both Neither	Husband Wife Both Neither	Husband Wife Both Someone Else	
Clean Bathrooms	Husband Wife Both Neither	Husband Wife Both Neither	Husband Wife Both Someone Else	
Car Maintenance	Husband Wife Both Neither	Husband Wife Both Neither	Husband Wife Both Someone Else	
Getting	Husband	Husband	Husband	

Getting Along

Kids Ready in Morning	Wife Both Neither	Wife Both Neither	Wife Both Someone Else	
Cooking Meals	Husband Wife Both Neither	Husband Wife Both Neither	Husband Wife Both Someone Else	
	Husband Wife Both Neither	Husband Wife Both Neither	Husband Wife Both Someone Else	

Creating a Life

Many couples are disillusioned by the toll that family and friends can take on a young marriage. In African villages, young married couples are sent away to live alone for a year before returning to the village. This time alone is used to become "one." These ancient cultures understand how difficult it can be for couples to become team-minded if they are still surrounded with family and friends. These loved ones are often guilty, however well meaning, of continuing to treat the husband and wife like they did before they were married.

As an example, I remember the case of our friend Casey. Casey is the only child of some very wealthy doctors. She was a daughter any parent would be proud to have. Casey had always been their world and she theirs. However, when she married, she had become Peter's world and he became hers.

Fortunately for Casey and Peter, their families got along great. Unfortunately, the newlyweds hardly spent time alone because their families got along so well. In the first few vital years instead of learning to walk out life as a couple by resolving problems and making plans, Peter and Casey still resembled two college kids dating who just happened to live together instead of with their parents.

Creating a Life

When Casey and Peter had issues, they each called their respective parents. When they had money problems, their parents paid to fix them. And when they got frustrated with each other, they stayed at their parents' homes without the other spouse.

When these two "children" decided to have a baby, they hired a nanny and continued their routine of cohabitating as married people. After about seven years, Casey and Peter were bored with each other and wanted a divorce. This couple couldn't even really say why they wanted to divorce, except that they were "bored."

This is an extreme example of newlyweds not becoming "one," but it makes my point. If you don't *create* a life with your spouse you won't *have* a life with your spouse. It is very easy to just continue on with your family as you did before marriage, and most well meaning friends and family members will let you do so, but this is not how you create a life.

Friends come to rely upon each other because of the time spent building the relationship. So, do your spouse a favor and put in the work to build your friendship with him or her. No spouse wants to be second in his or her spouse's eyes. Now, I am not suggesting that married people should throw away their friends and family, but I am suggesting that boundaries be set and priorities be determined—especially in the first few years.

Herb and I once talked with a couple, Jim and Tammy, who had been married about five years. Tammy was always angry because Jim worked a lot and didn't have much free time to spend with her. When Jim did get some free time, he usually spent it with his best buddy watching a football game. To Jim, his behavior was not a big deal. He felt that since he worked so hard he should be able to unwind with his lifetime buddy. Jim felt that Tammy wasn't as much fun or relaxing to be with as his buddy. This perspective really hurt Tammy, but she accepted it. So, Tammy had a life with her friends and Jim had a life with his buddy; the rest of the time Jim and Tammy spent their time at work. After five years of this lifestyle cohabitating as a married couple but not having a life as "one," Tammy wanted a divorce. Jim was shocked.

The pattern is the same for both of these two examples of newlywed couples: if we fail to plan at life, we plan to fail at life. Marriage is work. In Tammy and Jim's case, Jimmy had not given Tammy the chance to be his new best buddy. He hadn't carved out a priority space for Tammy to occupy in their new life.

Many new couples are afraid to change their relationships with their friends just to please their spouses. Without prioritizing a new spouse, however, trust and acceptance are lost. And the reality is that your friends and family should expect change to happen when you announce your engagements. Your single friends expect you to change: they expect the late nights to end, and they expect your spouse to become your main priority. But they will not change their behaviors until <u>you</u> set the new boundaries.

Creating a Life

Have you and your spouse set appropriate boundaries within which you are becoming one another's best friend? Have you clarified how and when your family and friends can engage with the two of you differently, now that you're married? It may feel a bit awkward in the beginning, but trust me: the two of you <u>must</u> make time to create a life together as "one." After you and your spouse become a team, you can always reset your boundaries a bit more open, but at that point your loved ones will see you differently.

The risk of not setting boundaries, however, is that within five years you and your amazing spouse can be divorcing like Jim and Tammy or Casey and Peter. The choice is yours. Are you ready to put in some more effort to learning to love your marriage? I hoped you would say, "Yes!" Below are some ideas for setting your initial boundaries as a couple committed to a long life together.

How to Build a Boundary

- **Create your own family traditions.** Too often families dictate holidays, birthdays, and celebration schedules and activities. Don't fall into this trap. Create your own. For traditional families this will be difficult. My mama's family is such a family: we have a tradition for everything. We travel to my grandmother's house for Christmas; to the aunts and uncles' homes for Thanksgiving; and to a family reunion in July....so forth and so on. Herb and I, however, had to break with all of my mama's family traditions during our first year of marriage in order to lay our own foundation and to include Herb's parents in our schedule. My mama's family didn't like not seeing me at every function, but they now recognize and love how blessed my family with Herb is as a result of my husband and I creating appropriate boundaries as we live out our loving marriage.

- **Have a regularly scheduled Date Night.** Schedule time every one or two weeks just for you as a couple. No friends. No family. No kids. Alternate between activities that interest one another, or experiment with something new neither of you had ever considered. Maybe you are not much into art, but a nice evening walk through an art gallery district can be a low-cost way to share your observations about the art, the people, or the weather. Even if you never do it again, you will be learning more about what your spouse does and doesn't like. If Jim had done this regularly with Tammy, he could have also still hung out with his buddy because Tammy would not have questioned her importance to Jim who had vowed to be with her until death.

- **When problems arise, consult God and then each other.** God is always wiser than you or anyone else. Start with Him. Then work with your spouse. If outside counsel is needed, seek it together. So the next time you don't know how to resolve a debt, pray over it with your spouse and then discuss it together before one of you calls dad. Google it together, if necessary, but learn to rely upon each other. I'm not saying not to get dad's opinion, but the priority is: God, your efforts, your spouse, and then outsiders. Diligence to this sequence will reinforce the wise boundaries you and your spouse are establishing for your life together.

- **Agree to not discuss each other's problems or shortcomings with friends and family.** This is huge and goes a long way toward honoring and respecting your spouse and your home. If you must share each other's issues with family, share them with your spouse's family and not your own. For example, if I have issues with Herb then I can call his dad. (I don't do this anymore, but I did in the beginning of our marriage.) Whatever I say about Herb to his dad will be understood and forgiven. On the contrary, if I were to talk to my mama about Herb's shortcomings, she might never forget my perception of his weakness and she may inadvertently treat him with less respect. Despite mama's love for Herb, she would always have a higher priority to protect my best interest.

- **Freely give each other the space and freedom to make boundary adjustments while maintaining your own individuality.** What?! Does that sound like a contradiction of everything I just said? It might, but it's not. Think about it, change takes time. We change step-by-step instead of all at once. After you set the boundaries, each of you will have to adjust, as well as all of your loved ones. For me, this was very difficult because I am a social butterfly, but my husband was not. After nineteen years, however, we are in balance with one another, not in perfection but far more than we thought possible. But it took time. In the beginning, Herb and I each struggled with our boundary to not discuss each other with family and friends. We were both used to sharing everything with our loved ones.

These are five suggestions for setting boundaries of your young marriage. Herb and I have used these types of boundaries. Along the way, we sometimes made mistakes...and you will too. Your humanity is real, and so is your spouse's. Reward the effort of your spouse, expect the mistakes, and give mercy and grace. After a little while, your hard work will pay off.

At first, it may not *look* like anything is different, but I encourage you to celebrate each time you and your spouse follow-through on protecting each of these boundaries. Even a high-five, or a word of encouragement will reinforce your new behaviors to one another.

Remember, your life together may begin just as a farmer plants a small seed in the ground. Even though you may not see any growth in a couple of days, the roots are growing deeper each time there's a bit of rain and sunshine. In a few weeks, you will have a healthy stalk of corn. And, then, you'll be partying with plenty of delicious corn on the cob. Start planting today, so you can celebrate sooner rather than later.

Now, here are action items for your next scheduled conversation with your spouse. As a piece of advice, do NOT consider this a date night. Instead, use it as a planning session to a lifetime of excellent date nights and traditions as you continue to create a life together as "one." The following table is just a sample of how you might plan out your boundaries. There is no "right" or "wrong" answer. As much as anything, the value comes in communicating about these important aspects of your married life.

Dying to Become One

Creating our life as "one"

Boundary				When? Under what conditions?
Family Traditions	*Christmas Eve: Her*	*Christmas Morning: Our House*	*Christmas Evening: His Mom's*	*This works for this year. We will always seek to keep Christmas Morning at our house. We will look around September each year to refine each holiday season as the larger family evolves.*
Date Nights	**1st Tue and 3rd Fri of each month**	*Each spouse takes responsibility for one night's plans for each month. We commit to planning to please the other person even more than ourselves.*	**Budget: $50 for Fri and $25 for Tue nights**	*If the wife is planning the activities, the husband takes responsibility to coordinate child care and vice-versa.*
Resolving Problems	**We commit to pray with each other every day, especially**	*We will take some alone time to consider what God is saying, before speaking with the other person.*	Together, we will determine if/how/with whom to ask questions.	*We commit to NOT discuss these problems with anyone else until we*

	as problems arise.			have both agreed on how to proceed.
Discussing Problems	See Resolving Problems!	We will not speak dishonorably about the other person outside our family.		If one of us does need a different perspective, even after prayer and talking to the other person, we commit to speaking with the "designated" parent / friend to which we both agree.
Graceful Boundaries	See Resolving Problems!	We will practice flexibility and patience with one another, as well as with our family and friends as we all learn to adapt to these changing boundaries.		

Sharing: We & Us

The third question about becoming "one" that I will address is, "Are we supposed to share everything?" The question about sharing is a tough one, even now after so many years of marriage. On one hand I'd like to dogmatically say, "Yes, share everything!" On the other hand, I recognize that every situation is different. When Herb and I got married, we had nothing to lose by sharing. I mean we were broke, busted, and disgusted. So, over the years, as we acquired things, everything was "ours." In this way, it was a blessing to be broke in the beginning because I wasn't territorial about "my" stuff.

When other couples ask me this question, then, I ask them about their dreams, goals, and fears. These hold the root to the answer of whether you should share. When Herb and I first started out, we were counseled by many well-meaning people to get separate accounts. In this way, they said, if the other spouse doesn't live up to your expectations, you'll have a nest egg in which to leave on. Coming from divorced parents, I understood that sometimes marriages do fail. Herb's parents were still together so he had an entirely different view on the issue.

Now, for us, we dreamed of growing old together, our goals included things like leaving a legacy for our children, and our

Sharing: We & Us

fear was being divorced. Neither one of us wanted to invest in anything that prepared us—or protected us—just in case we divorced. That was not the direction we wanted to head.

Here is an example to consider. Herb and I were once approached at a marriage retreat by another couple. They had each been married before and they were planning to get married, so they were attending the retreat. They both already had separate homes, accounts, and children. Anyway, they wondered what we thought of them keeping their homes and buying a third home together...just in case things didn't work out. Tough already, right?

Now, I can admit that their suggestion has *some* logic and that it is rational and wise, but *only to a point*. I mean, if you think you have a 50/50 chance of being divorced again, why wouldn't you keep a spare home to live in should things not work out? But on the other hand, we cannot overlook the *purpose* of those spare homes. They are seeds for a future divorce! Intentions mean *everything*! What are your goals, dreams, and fears? These dictate and pave the road to every action you take.

Another example can be found in the scriptures. Maybe you remember when the early church was being formed, after Jesus had returned to heaven. If you don't, then I encourage you to read the Book of Acts. Anyway, in the early days, everyone was being persecuted for believing in and professing Christ. All they had was the Lord and each other. So the early Church decided to care for

Dying to Become One

each other, help each other, and cover each other. They took *all* they had and *shared* it with each other.

And think about it: the Church, the Body of Christ, *still exists* today. I believe that their long-ago, simple act of sharing and loving each other more than they loved themselves, planted a seed of longevity that Satan himself has not been able to tear apart. Even today, you can find Christians and Christian churches of every variety, sharing and giving to one another.

So, to answer your question, I encourage you to share for the long-term success of your marriage: this commitment is good seed for your future together as "one." There is no "I" in "team." Practically, start as early as the wedding day practicing the words "we" and "us." Start getting comfortable with the feel of those words on your lips. And remember that material stuff is temporary and replaceable.

Love, on the other hand, is a priceless commodity. If you lose anything in love, God is capable of replacing. If that doesn't prick your heart, think of all that Jesus sacrificed for us: he *shared* all he had by having faith that we would not take his kind offering as a sign of weakness.

Do these examples answer the question about sharing yourselves with one another?

Sharing: We & Us

Learning to Share

I challenge you two to consider what you are currently sharing and what you are not. Also, communicate with each other about how that sharing or not sharing is going to benefit the two of you as becoming "one" for eternity. The sample table on the next page can facilitate your conversation.

What do we share?

Item	Do we share?	Can we share more?	How?	What's the long-term benefit?
Money	Yes No Sometimes	Yes	Consolidate 100% of our money into a joint account.	It will build trust and encourage us to communicate more about how and when to spend money. That communication will help us grow as "one."
Car/s	Yes No Sometimes			
Time	Yes No Sometimes			
Problems	Yes No Sometimes			
Successes	Yes No Sometimes			
	Yes No Sometimes			

Sharing: We & Us

Learning about Faithfulness

Now that I have given you the same advice I would give a newlywed couple sitting in my living room about how to become "one," let me also share some of my life experiences about learning to become "one" with Herb. First, Herb and I had our share of issues to resolve as newlyweds, some of which I will share with you. Additionally, we struggled with our life purposes. We even stumbled on our walk with God. And, as individuals, we continued to battle issues from our past. But, because we had committed to daily prayers, Herb and I tackled each new challenge with God in the middle of our daily prayers. And God kept showing us new ways to do things.

Partnering with my husband and God helped me in even some of the most personal challenges I had experienced even as a young girl terrified by dreams. While I had been comforted when my Aunt confirmed that she, too, "saw things," I did not always know how to process my crazy dreams. With the guidance Herb and I received by praying with the Lord each day, I came to learn that dreams are often heaven-sent to encourage, guide, or warn people.

Dying to Become One

At other times, however, dreams can also represent enemy tactics to overcome the God-given destiny of people. By reading *The Divine Revelation of Hell*, which I highly recommend if this is an issue for you, I now recognize that some of my dreams came directly from the gates of hell. While my book is not about these types of spiritual warfare, I share the example that partnering with my husband and God brought new understanding that I could not have gained any other way. In essence, because of a difficult situation that neither Herb or I had ever experienced before, we *had* to trust God *and* trust one another to keep ourselves growing as "one."

Now, I ask you to trust me that there is *great* value in a couple learning to become "one."

Even as Herb and I were strengthening our marriage through examples of complex spiritual issues, however, I began to grow very dissatisfied with life. Our life was very stable at this point: Herb and I were both working, the kids were doing great, we were financially fine, and we did not have any intense pressures. But I was still unsettled emotionally. For a while, I rationalized to myself that I just didn't know how to handle so much peace after years of intense pressures. But that excuse allowed me to ignore the nagging feeling for only so long.

With that nagging, we entered another season of testing and growth. This kind of testing and growth is not easy to read

Learning about Faithfulness

about or even write about. On the contrary, it's the facts and realities of marriage that most church people don't want to discuss. Despite that, I will discuss the challenge and how we overcame it. I choose to share it because I am convinced that my ability to overcome is based on God's goodness. And, since he's no respecter of persons, I pray that you will be blessed by learning how to overcome unexpected problems.

Life is difficult, but I realize I learn best from people who have actually experienced those challenges and learned from them. For me, I hate when a trainer at the gym who has always been a size 2 and never had any children approaches me. I mean that trainer can't help me.

Instead, I appreciate the coaches and trainers who have actually conquered something: they've been fat and overcame their emotional eating; they used to be broke and overcame poverty; or they used to be academically challenged and then they worked hard and learned some things. The Bible describes these kinds of leaders as "more than conquerors" because they have known defeat and fought for victory.

Moses is one of these Bible leaders who started out on top of life, living in a mansion with servants and everything he could have ever asked for because he was the adopted son of Pharaoh's sister. But when Moses started to actually walk with God, his circumstances humbled him. He ran away from Egypt because he murdered a man, served as a shepherd for his father-in-law's flocks, and stuttered even to himself in a desert wasteland. But from this humble place, Moses learned to trust God's guidance and to overcome his insecurities and past failures. Not only did God have Moses speak for him to Pharaoh, but God allowed Moses to lead hundreds of thousands of people out of captivity. By trusting God's voice, Moses learned to stand against all odds, receiving victory not just for himself, but also for his entire race.

These are the men and women I aspire to learn from and to emulate. None of them, so far, has been perfect. My husband and I fit into this category of overcoming conquerors.

As I mentioned earlier, I misdiagnosed the nagging feeling that began to arrive when our married life seemed more stable. At first, I thought it was boredom with the good life. The routine of our responsibilities and commitments for each other, the kids, the house, church, etc., just wasn't exciting to me anymore. Then I thought it was because I didn't like my job, so I started a side business in addition to my job. As a matter of fact, I started several businesses…and all of them were failures.

Because of my independent nature, I actually started most of my business ventures without Herb, because he had a job and he didn't have my desire to conquer the world: he was content. In my heart, I grew to despise him for this disinterest in my vision to dominate the world. As a couple, we had always done everything together since those first library dates, but now I was doing something alone. Striving to succeed on these new adventures

Learning about Faithfulness

without my husband and best friend made me feel even more angry and disgruntled.

The business that had the largest impact on our marriage was my promotions business. It was fun and I got to do a lot of traveling and socializing as I focused all of my energy in helping other people achieve their dreams and visions, in contrast to how I saw Herb sitting alone at home. In short, the primary issue was that I was away from home too often.

Over time, this new lifestyle as a professional promoter became more "real" to me than my home life. I mean, I loved my husband and my kids, but I also loved being "free" to do creative things. As with most things that get out of balance, being away from home began to take a higher priority than my own family. And, when confronted by this fact, I began to resent being married.

I felt like my marriage was a weight that was tying me down. It wasn't that I didn't love Herb; I just thought I didn't love marriage, anymore. I missed the freedom of flying through different circles of life. I felt that I had a whole new bubble to conquer, but was being held back by this "institution" of marriage. I believed I was required to go home when I wanted to fly to New York. Being a parent was wonderful—unless it interfered with one of my stylish and exciting promotions events. I was selfish and unrepentant and my silent fight for freedom began here.

Actually, I was being flat-out rebellious…to my commitments, my husband, and to God.

Looking back, I understand that the sins of my father were making themselves known to me. I understand that if I had talked about it with Herb we could have avoided many future hurts; but I chose not to talk about it. Instead, I smiled and played my role as a good wife and good mother while growing more and more distant from the family that I loved and had yearned for, though I was unable see it in this light at the time.

It would take years before I learned that I was never taught faithfulness. Books cannot teach faithfulness. Hearts have to be conditioned to submit to faithfulness. My heart had not yet made this transition to fully trust and commit to other people, even in the midst of boredom or difficulties. I wanted what I had grown accustomed to before my family: having relationships and my freedom, too. I was definitely selfish, but I was ignorant and blinded to the truth of the matter.

The process of becoming "one," in truth, is not pretty. It takes years to die to one's selfishness so the process of truly living, as "one" can be possible with another person. But I did not recognize or understand either the process or the future benefit of being consistent in learning to live as "one" with my husband.

Herb and I had died a lot to our immature selves under the earlier pressures of our young marriage, but I have more recently learned that each person can be sharper and more focused during the heat of the fight of surviving against the world as a united

Learning about Faithfulness

couple. Unfortunately, it is during the slow periods of life—when people are resting and off their guard—that the enemy's temptations creep in.

As long as we were united in our fighting other situations—such as my crazy dreams—Herb and I were focused on the same "battlefield." Now, in a peaceful season of our marriage, we were like Samson when he grew tired and laid his head in Delilah's lap. After what Samson thought would be a quick nap, he awoke to find his power had been stripped from him by the very one he lay with.

Herb and I had fought the good fight for many years, but the time came for us to fight our own desires and ourselves. If we could win this new, internal fight, we could leave our old selves behind...but this battle hadn't been won yet. Hindsight is twenty-twenty; but in the midst of unknown territory, vision is blurry and out-of-focus.

The only relationship on earth that can be compared to marriage is a believer's relationship with Christ. Receiving him in one's heart, however, is only the spiritual transformation, a beginning. Over time, if we will allow Jesus to do the work, we are changed into the image of him on the outside as well. But this transition isn't instantaneous.

Marriage is very similar. When each of you says, "I do", you become legally married to each other. But that is just the beginning of your marriage. The transformation to "oneness" as a couple is a journey. Just as the spiritual transition requires submitting ourselves to Christ and his ways of doing things, there is value in submitting ourselves to our spouse and "our" way of doing things.

I have learned that it is a lot easier in both situations when I am more obedient than rebellious. In my relationship with Christ, I come up under subjection to Jesus' will and way. He becomes Lord over my life. As I seek to honor him with my life, I am forever changed. As I honor my spouse and our marriage relationship, we are also forever changed into the image of "one" in Christ, who is perfect unity.

But in this particular season of my marriage to Herb, I was not being honorable. Instead, I was seeking to create my own image, and in that there is always chaos. Living God's way produces peace, but I was not feeling peaceful.

From my perspective, I had given up freedom to fly whichever way the wind took me when I married. I wish I could tell you God simply intervened and gave me superhuman powers to resolve the tensions and the conflicts, but that's just not what happened.

Like all situations in life, I had to choose. I had to choose to cook when I didn't want to. I had to choose to get up in the middle of the night to meet the kids' needs, even if I was tired. Choices!

Learning about Faithfulness

God gives us a choice. He constantly put me in remembrance of the covenant I had made with him to love my husband. He also reminded me of my vow to my grandmother to be a good wife. These memories were enough to keep me from running away, as my dad had done from his own battle with faithfulness.

But my immature view of faithfulness was not sufficient to make me happy on the inside. I felt obligated and put-upon. I prayed constantly for relief from the craving for my freedom.

I prayed to stay faithful.

And God answered my prayer.

I do believe, though, that the Lord has a sense of humor. In return for my prayers, Herb and I moved into a house directly across the street from my dad. Of all the places in the world, why did God move us across the street from my dad, who continues to be unfaithful to those he loves?!?

The short version of how we lived so near my dad is simple. On a routine visit to my dad, who lived with his wife of over twenty years, dad had spoken with Herb concerning an investment property across the street. In just a few words Herb heard how dad had bought the house and how he offered that we could live there for free for a while. Herb became very excited about the potentially dramatic decrease in our monthly expenditures, so Herb accepted my dad's offer.

What?! Shock is the simplest word to describe the confusion I sensed about living so close to the man who had contributed to my gene pool, but had been so absent and transient through my mama's other two marriages and my tormented life. I came to refer to my dad as a "rolling stone." He was good-looking, suave, smart, and interested in my opinions during the short and rare conversations we had had during my childhood. My dad was at times even generous. But, he was as emotionally hurtful as I and my ex-lover had been. There wasn't a bone of faithfulness in that man's body!

And, frankly, his unfaithfulness was evident every day that we lived across the street from my dad. He may have been married to that wife for over twenty years, but having a marriage license does not predict with whom one sleeps. It was easy for me to understand why my mama had stayed married to my dad for such a short time.

Herb and I lived across the street from my dad for only a year, but it seemed like an eternity! As I observed my dad from the front-row seat that God had put me in, I grew to detest what I had become and myself. I hated my dad's version of freedom and unfaithfulness that was running through my veins.

By seeing more clearly how I was headed towards a destructive life of selfish misery, I realized I needed a change. I determined in my heart, instead, that I would discover the true freedom like that of my Aunt Irene and Uncle Thelbert. They were

Learning about Faithfulness

joyful and hopeful, living and enjoying a free life together as a happy couple.

Once I realized that I had choices about the path my adult life would take, I preferred to spend time with Aunt Irene and Uncle Thelbert. Just being around them gave me peace and encouragement. Watching them interact gave me a different vision of married life than what I had witnessed with all of my parents and their angry or unfaithful relationships. By the grace of God, I learned I could make faithful choices within my marriage.

To help grow me even further, the Lord sent Herb and me to a church not far from our new home across the street from my dad. This church was filled with strong married folks. We took part in their marriage ministry, and that year we attended our first marriage conference. If you've never been to a marriage conference, you must find an anointed one and go immediately. It will bless your marriage beyond belief!

I remember how this particular church marriage conference changed our married lives. I would give you all the details, but that is one of the pluses of such a conference: it's private. It's like the marketing campaign for Las Vegas: what happens there stays there. What is spoken in transparency in front of all the other couples is not spoken of outside the conference.

I will say this, however: I learned that people who have been married fifty years still have problems with becoming "one," still misunderstand one another, and are still looking for their place and purpose in each other's life. Not every couple, of course, has these issues after so long, but many of them do.

At the marriage conference, I learned that the love that I shared with Herb—even among those senior marriages—was a priceless rare treasure! I learned the value of my friendship with Herb. And I began to see that—despite my internal issues—Herb and I had indeed been given a gift of special grace as a couple. The pastor of this new church even mentioned seeing the spiritual red bow around our family that I spoke of earlier.

During the conference, Herb and I both had opportunities to speak to the participants. We spoke from our hearts. I was transparent about of my desire to be free and how God had used my dad's life to bring me back down to earth. In between sessions, other couples began to approach Herb and me.

Some of the people who approached us were church leaders whom we respected. We were surprised, however, that their words mirrored those spoken by our friends and associates in college. These older Christian couples inquired of the apparent stability, love, unwavering friendship, and ease with one another that they saw in Herb and me. We were shocked, because of the daily struggles in which we lived our lives. Yet, by the grace of God, these strangers were unable to see my internal desires for freedom or Herb's feelings of inadequacy. It was as if the Lord was

Learning about Faithfulness

hiding our frailties from other people, even though Herb and I had each spoken transparently about our issues to the group.

It really goes without saying that Herb and I left the conference renewed and changed. We were beginning to see ourselves as God saw us. Additionally, that time of reflection enabled us to recognize the growth we had already accomplished.

While I should have better appreciated the God-given role of reflecting the strengths of marriage to other people, I was still not yet mature enough to completely trust God and Herb and lay down my own self will.

After the church marriage conference, Herb and I returned to our life in the house across the street from my dad. I grew more and more disgusted with my dad's life, but I continued to battle with my own desires for freedom. While the conference hadn't "cured" me, it did show me that my battle for my family was worth fighting.

I also gained a new understanding of Paul's words when he said in the Bible that we must work out our salvation with *much* fear and trembling. It takes time; everything worth having takes time to achieve. Maturing is a process.

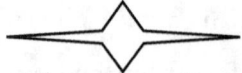

I believe that the Lord is a great father who does not hold us accountable for things that we have yet to learn. Like with my own children, I don't punish them for things I've yet to teach them how to do. That would just be wrong.

So, looking back, I understand that I was receiving an increasing dose of faithfulness both by living across the street from my dad and by attending the marriage conference. Yet, despite the growing *wisdom* of faithfulness, I had yet to gain *understanding* on how to walk out faithfulness. There are two pieces of maturing in an area of life. In the Book of Proverbs, the sage counselor advises that we get wisdom *and* understanding.

Thus, at this point in my life of learning to grow as "one" with Herb, I acknowledged that I had to fight at any cost against a desire for flight for incomplete freedom. What I didn't understand, yet, was why my desire to run was so great or how to get rid of it. It would take a future trip to the desert for me to learn about generational curses and the sins of the father.

Thanks be to God and his faithfulness, however, that I finally realized that it was wrong to go my own way. I was beginning to mature in his ways. I didn't know, yet, how to stop the thoughts or desires that seemed so contrary to God's ways. I still lacked the keys to real deliverance so that I could more maturely become "one" with my husband. Even still, I was growing in an understanding of God and his faithfulness to me, and I began to trust that he would continue to teach me how to be truly free *and* to live as "one" with my husband.

Learning to be Faithful

Before I continue with finding your God-given purposes, I challenge you as a couple to consider the following topics. Start

Learning about Faithfulness

individually and then schedule time to share your perspectives with your spouse. Again, do NOT consider this important conversation as a Date Night!

1. What "nags" at you when you are alone? Is it a weakness in your spouse? Or just dissatisfaction within yourself? Have you discussed it with your spouse? Why or why not?
2. What does faithfulness look like to you? What does God's word say about it? Do these two sources look the same, yet? Or is there room for growth on your side? If there is room for maturity in your faithfulness, how might you improve your ability to understand or "walk out" a faithful attitude?
3. If you want to grow in your faithfulness, how would you like your spouse to help you? Do you desire more encouragement or support from him/her while you practice being more faithful? Or is there a tender spot in your heart on this topic that you would like your spouse to protect and guard you as you grow in this area?
4. Have you ever considered attending a marriage retreat? Does your pastor have any recommendations? Or is there someone in your church whom you admire and trust that you and your spouse can spend some time with the more experienced couple? Ask them and see if the four of you can make plans to begin talking about these important subjects.

Finding Your God-Given Purpose

Several years passed for Herb and me: we excelled in our careers, acquired more finances than we needed, and strengthened our relationship. Yet, I still struggled with my life-long desire to "fly," even though we had actually relocated from Texas to a new home in Iowa.

Even looking back at that time, I remember not feeling happy, despite the tangible achievements my family and I had experienced. It's strange how I had begun to see my inner yearning more like a void that I was learning to live with while the "good life" surrounded me. Sure, I loved my family and found contentment with them, but my spirit was not yet at peace.

Herb and I regularly attended church and we consistently prayed as a couple, but something was "off." I felt like I was missing something, even though it looked like I was living within my dreams of freedom, riches, and a healthy family. Herb and I were blessed with wonderful children. We were prosperous (at least more prosperous than during my childhood). And I had learned to become "one" with Herb, so I was loving my freedom *with* Herb.

But I still felt like I had somehow missed my true purpose in life.

At the time, I was working a lot; frankly, I was a workaholic. A wise woman might have spent many hours praying with God about how to overcome the workaholic tendencies, but I don't have that testimony. Neither Herb nor I recognized at that time the value of dedicating one's self to that kind of transformation through prayer. I thought I didn't have that kind of time to "sit around and just pray," and neither did Herb.

Because Herb and I were praying daily, however, I was becoming more sensitive to my thoughts and emotions. Unfortunately, that nagging feeling of somehow being "off" stuck around. I believe now that the Lord allowed the nagging to continue so that I would one day seek his wisdom about it.

The discomfort in this one area of my life got so big in my life that I finally had to stop, look around, and realize that I had to change my actions if I wanted to overcome the lack of peace. Frankly, the scenario of how and why I finally slowed down to listen to God should be in another book, but suffice it to say that the Lord *knows* how to "maketh" me to lie down in green pastures.

Finally slowing down from my normally busy life, I lay in my green pastures. There, I had time to ask myself if I was doing all that God wanted me to do. More importantly, I also asked myself if I was, instead, just doing what I wanted to do; and that was a more difficult question to answer.

It may sound wonderfully deep to someone else that I was asking these questions, but living through that self-evaluation—and being completely transparent before the all-knowing God—was not so deep, and definitely not fun. Instead, that alone time with God was heart wrenching! Today, however, I am so thankful that I learned that God is faithful to answer our heart's cry when we will "be still and know that he is God." He really does have the answer to every single question about our lives!

God revealed to me that *I* was the source of my lack of peace. Ouch! As I reflected on my past choices and actions, it became crystal clear that I had selfishly chosen to prefer myself over other people or over God's preference for what I did and how I did it. As I said, it was a painful time, especially because of the pride that I began to realize existed in my life.

Thankfully, however, God is also merciful. He had not needed to have someone stand up in a public place to announce to the whole world that I had not been fully obedient to his wishes for me. Instead, he made them clear to me in our one-on-one time, but *only* after I finally slowed down enough to seek his perspective.

It was in that private turmoil that I finally recognized that the Lord was calling me to live fully, completely, and sacrificially for him. He was asking me to lay down my own preferences and my own will to learn how to trust him in every situation. He was

Finding Your God-Given Purpose

asking me to find my one, true purpose only through my relationship with Jesus Christ. Despite my previous weaknesses, selfishness, and pride, it was as if the Lord reached down to my heart and mind, washed away my mistakes, and asked, "Will you be <u>completely</u> mine?"

Today, I am so glad that I said, "Yes!"

A victorious marriage can only be achieved if each person finds his or her purpose in Christ. Herb and I have chosen to make God the center of our marriage, just as we have chosen as individuals to allow him to be Lord of our lives.

When we allow God to be the foundation of our relationship, shouldn't we be doing what the Lord would have us do? Because he's Lord of our lives, then he's Lord of our marriage, and our marriage should become a reflection of his purpose for our lives. He has a purpose for each marriage and for each of us individually.

As I came to better understand what God was telling me in that one-on-one time, I learned that the void existed in my life because I was not yet living up to all of my God-given potential. I had expected that once I obtained the desired money and family that my life would be fulfilled.

Instead, I just felt disappointed and shouted, "OK, now what? Is this it?"

In his kind and personal way, God revealed to me that I had met the earthly needs of my flesh and mind, but that my spirit still lacked the only fulfillment that would suffice: to know and walk in my purpose in Christ.

I began to wonder why I was born. Questions that had never previously dawned in my brain began to plague me constantly. God has designed each of us to play a specific part in the Kingdom of God, but I did not yet know my part. It was this disconnect between what God had called me to be and my as-yet unrealized living of that role that created that void in my spirit. Thankfully, God began to explain to me that even my desire to conquer the world, or to be queen of the world, was actually a desire given to me by Christ.

But, I wondered, for what purpose would he want me to rule the world? At the time, I was a manager over an Information Technology (IT) department. I wondered if that was my God-given purpose, but it didn't seem likely.

Once I knew what question needed to be answered, I realized that I just needed to be steered in the right direction, and deep down I knew that the clarity of my assignment from God could only come from him. While I, even as a wise human cannot see the full picture of my life, God can. As much as Herb loved me and wanted to help, he also did not have enough wisdom or knowledge to help me.

No one could help me find my God-given purpose but the Lord, himself.

Unfortunately, because of my spiritual immaturity and impatience, I did not wait on the Lord to give me more clarity on my purpose. Instead, I continued to practice unwise behaviors that appeared to meet my short-term needs for "peace." It would have been wiser if I had continued to "be still and know that he is God" while he trained me to live my life his way, but I ended up getting lost in sin, drugs, and depression.

As I grew more depressed with my lack of fulfillment, I began drinking alcohol and smoking weed. Of course, this shift in my lifestyle didn't happen all at once. Like most tricks from the enemy, it was a gradual slide away from his best for my life. And, because of my childhood family, some of the behaviors were easier to adopt than others.

At first, drinking and smoking were very casual and infrequent activities. Then, one day, I realized that I was smoking every day. Because neither my parents nor I had ever been much drinkers, I only drank alcohol on the weekends; frankly, drinking wasn't in my blood. Smoking marijuana, however, was much more familiar to me.

From the time I was thirteen years old until I left for college, I had watched my dad smoke a joint like other people smoke cigarettes: all day long. My dad was a professional engineer who wore suits every day to work, and I never saw him display any "druggy" behavior. He was always functional and presentable, despite his consistent marijuana smoking. Based on my dad's outward appearance, I would not have believed he was addicted to pot except that I had watched him consistently with my own eyes.

My dad's actions and behaviors made quite an impression on me. I learned that the effects of marijuana could be controlled by some people, and that motivated me to figure out how to hide my weed smoking from other people. I also learned that marijuana affected me differently than how I perceived that other hard drugs could take over a person's life, rendering them ineffective. Because neither my dad nor I *appeared* to be ineffective, I rationalized that I was in control of my pot smoking.

And, yet, I was eventually smoking a joint every night before bed. Arriving home from work as an IT manager, I fed the kids, prepared them for bed, read to them, prayed with them, and then I would smoke weed as soon as the kids were asleep. During these times, I believed that smoking helped me relax and that it put away the anxieties of my dull life.

On the weekends, however, Herb and I threw parties and filled our lives with other financially successful people who had no relationship with God. For a period of two years, Herb and I kept up all of our wise routines that God had established—like praying, reading the Bible, etc.—but we added in partying, smoking, and drinking, whenever *we* decided it would be good.

Remember, I was struggling with how to learn to live my life God's preferred way. And, frankly, I wasn't yet succeeding at living God's way. Unfortunately, as the drugs and alcohol dulled my senses, I believed the lie that the void of my life was no longer in my heart. And, despite our "oneness" and our commitments to God, it didn't help that Herb was also struggling with the exact same lie and poor lifestyle choices.

Because of my distorted view of reality, I believed that the drugs and alcohol gave me a temporary peace and that they served a valuable distraction from the depression that was invading my life. I never even considered that I had a drug problem until one night when my young daughter wasn't feeling well. When I needed to change my nightly routine to care for my daughter, as any mother should, I remember growing frustrated: why couldn't she get better more quickly?

I remember thinking, "Now I'll never get to smoke tonight!"

When I recognized myself thinking this way, I suddenly "came to myself." I realized that I had created a monster within myself who was deceiving me daily. In an instant, I remembered how harshly I had judged my own mama when she had struggled with drugs during my own childhood.

Did I really have the capacity to travel down the same path as my mama and her issues? Not only did I begin to understand my mama's choices better than ever, I recognized that God is the only true judge of each person. I quickly repented to God for how I had previously judged my mama.

I also recognized that God was the only one who could help me overcome the roots of the issues that had deceived me so much about the depression and the drugs and alcohol. I did not stop smoking immediately, but I did finally ask God for his help. In the beginning, I struggled each night when my sober mind was flooded with thoughts of how pointless my life was. I believed that my life was purposeless.

During those two years of depression and drug use, I had created habitual behaviors of avoiding the state of my life. Overcoming this daily denial was difficult, and I failed many attempts to quit the drug use. A few months later, however, I finally had the strength to quit, but only with the help of God.

Like any good father, the Lord gave me experiences that allowed me to break through these debilitating thoughts. For example, there was a time when I sat in my car with my mama. We had been out shopping and as I was dropping her home, we began to talk about life.

Finding Your God-Given Purpose

I remember I began to cry, and words poured out of me that told the story of my hopelessness and despair over life. I told my mama how I had wanted the freedom, family, and riches, how I had received them, but now I hated it all! None of it made me happy, not even my own family. In that moment of brokenness, I—the supposedly strong and independent queen of the world—asked my very human mama to help me.

And she did!

Mama asked me a few questions that day, and she shared from her heart. "Nisha," she asked, "what makes you happy? You know, life isn't about money. Oh, money helps but it's more than that. It's about discovering yourself and learning why you are here."

Mama then told me that I was the best parent she'd ever known. She said I seemed really passionate about my kids and helping people. Mama encouraged me because she recognized what an amazing marriage Herb and I had, especially because of everything we had successfully overcome to that point. She then counseled me to focus on doing what I loved.

With tears rolling down my eyes, I asked her the deep question that had tormented me all of those years, "Mama, what's my purpose?"

I didn't know what I was expecting, but I knew that I needed a life line, some words of hope that would help anchor me and secure me from all of the battles I had been encountering each night in my head.

"Baby," she answered me, "I don't know exactly what your purpose is, but I can tell you confidently that God made you to be great!"

My mama continued with a story. "I remember the day you were born. I was standing in the room with mama and daddy, and all of a sudden, daddy was staring at something and tears were rolling down his eyes. I looked to see what had moved him to tears and then I saw you.

"You were only a few hours old, in your crib. You had propped yourself up on your arms and were looking around the room.

"My daddy said, 'Babies don't do that! This child has been sent here from the Lord to do something amazing.'

"And I just cried, and he cried."

As my mama spoke those amazing, prophetic words—passed to me through my mama from her daddy, we were both crying. I had heard this story before, but I was transformed in that instant. Maybe it was because I finally recognized the voice of God that had spoken through my grandfather all of those years ago. Maybe I could finally value my mother's heart and forgive her for the weaknesses I had experienced in her insecure parenting skills. Or maybe I had finally arrived at a point where I was actually willing to hear from God and leave my own selfish preferences to learn how to grow in his way of living my life.

Mama wisely counseled me to focus on my family, rather than chase after empty, workaholic management jobs. She encouraged me to pray about my purpose. She also told me to be obedient and to do the next right thing.

That may have been the best suggestion I have ever received. You know, suggesting that someone "do the next right thing" may be wiser than telling someone specifically what to do, because only God knows exactly what the next step should be in climbing out of the hole of despair and hopelessness that my own behaviors had put me in.

Mama's counsel also challenged me to "be still and know that he is God," until I had a clear understanding of what the "next thing" should be.

A second experience I had with God, as he was guiding me into a clearer understanding of my life purpose, happened one Sunday morning. Herb and I had returned to Texas from Iowa. Because we did not yet have a church home, I was lying in bed flipping through the television channels to find a church service to watch. I settled on Joel Osteen that day.

I'll never forget it: Pastor Joel began talking to my spirit about joy. He quoted the Psalms.

The LORD is my strength and my shield; my heart trusts in him, and he helps me.

My heart leaps for joy, and with my song I praise him.

Psalms 28:7

As my spirit heard God's word that day, my spirit actually leaped! While Pastor Joel preached, I asked God to give me His joy that strengthens, and I believe I have possessed it ever since!

At the time, I did not have words to explain the difference in how I felt. All I knew was that the previous night I had smoked weed (though much less frequently than before), and this night I was free! Today, I would explain that God imparted his grace and his power for me to overcome my difficult situation through his words spoken through that anointed minister of God.

Even after all these years, people testify that they sense a presence of extraordinary joy when they are around me and my family. I know confidently that I received God's supernatural joy that Sunday morning with Joel Osteen. While I have had periodic moments of doubts, despair, or depression since that special day, God's joy always overrides those evil voices and strengthens me to hope, to have faith in him and his word, and to step out in courage despite the visible obstacles!

I have shared in this chapter my intimate and debilitating struggles of being bound in the darkness of an enemy's lies while

Finding Your God-Given Purpose

going through the motions of life. Because of my parents' weaknesses to drugs and their delayed confirmation to me—as their child—that I had purpose in this world, I was snared in the lies that my life didn't matter. Because I had lived as a "mature" person from an early age, I had not been trained to recognize and overcome the negative thoughts of worthlessness that invaded my brain every night. And I rationalized that if I drank enough or smoked enough—as long as I didn't interfere with my powerful employment—that I could "erase" that nagging void in my heart.

But that it is no way to live!

Once I was delivered from depression and my coping mechanisms, it was as if the lights of truth went on in my mind about my God-given purpose, as well. I was no longer without direction. I had things to do!

And, you know what? My God-given purpose had been there all along. The lies I believed, however, had put that bright path into the shadows and I couldn't remember how to turn the lights back on to find it.

Remember when I told you couples kept coming to me and Herb for help, but we felt inadequate to assist them? Remember my dream about the couples that crowded our front lawn seeking help? Remember how other people testified to seeing an anointing on Herb, and me like a big red bow? Well, none of that had left me and it all had purpose...my God-given, life-worth-living purpose.

God wants me to help people love each other!

As the darkness of the evil thoughts was cleared from my brain, I got it! I had a purpose for living! I had abundant joy! And I started to recognize an even larger goal, a goal bigger than any I'd set before. The Lord has called my family to be instruments in his hands for the purpose of restoring families.

I am grateful for the opportunities the Lord has provided for me to minister into individuals who regain their sense of purpose, especially as they then learn to minister into their own families. I am honored that he has enabled Herb and me to minister into our own families, from which we now reap the Lord's abundant grace, mercy, and encouragement despite the challenges we all had when we were children. And now I am excited to see how the Lord is allowing my experiences and the wisdom he has imparted into me to minister to you, my reader.

So far, it's been a wonderful ride! And as you continue to seek out the Lord's way of living your life—both as an individual and as a couple—I am excited to learn of *your* wonderful ride with God.

In closing this chapter, the first thing I want to do is to impart into you the anointing to BE FREE! Jesus came to set the captives free. It is a promise to you. Do you believe that the word

Finding Your God-Given Purpose

is true? Trust me, I know. It is much better to be free of the enemy's lies and his tactics.

Oh, it might take you weeks or months to truly believe that God loves you and that his ways are always better. It took me several years to walk it out effectively. I stumbled and fell, but I did not quit. So don't you quit, either!

On the other hand, God is still in the miracle-working business. Just as Jesus turned regular water to wine in an instant, you can receive all of his grace, mercy, joy, and strength in an instant. BE JOYFUL!

God in heaven has a picture-perfect purpose he picked out just for you. Do you believe it? Do you want to know what it is?

As my mama told me, I may not know exactly what you're supposed to be doing with God. But I do know that you are called to BE GREAT! That's right. The Bible says that you are even supposed to do MORE MIRACLES than Jesus. What do you think about that?

So, if you do not already know more precisely what God's purpose is for you, it is up to you to ask him. Just like with me, he may tell you that there is a weakness or two in your character that he wants to help you with. But remember, he wants to *wash it all away* so that you and he can BE FREE, BE JOYFUL, BE GREAT, and DO MORE MIRACLES than Jesus.

Your purpose is not about the money, fame, or any of the earthly things you might be seeking. But it's more precious than gold. It has eternal value. It is the reason you were born.

Get still, know that he's God, and ask the King of the Universe why he put you on planet earth. What does he want you and your spouse to accomplish for the Kingdom of God? Knowing God's purpose for your lives will bless you as individuals and as an amazing couple of God.

BE BLESSED!

Learning to be Still

While most of the suggested exercises in this book are for you to communicate together as a couple, this exercise is designed for each of you to execute as individuals in partnership with God. After you have each made the time to "sit and pray," then consider repeating the process as a couple.

The point of this exercise is for you to learn to be still and to know that he is God. The God of the universe desires to reveal directly to you that you have a specific purpose. Will you listen for his "still small voice"?

1. Make a daily appointment with God in which you will be still. Put in on the calendar. Practice your faithfulness by keeping this appointment.
2. Choose a peaceful location. Maybe it's in a cozy chair in a corner, or in a guest bedroom, or on your porch at sunrise or sunset. Maybe you want to light a candle, dim the lights, or listen to soft music.
3. Have a Bible, a notepad, and a pen with you. You can make it a girly notebook with a purple pen if that makes you happy, but the most important point is to be ready to listen and to write what you hear.

Yes, to write what you hear.

Maybe being still and listening for the voice of God is something new for you, but trust me, the God of the universe who spoke the world into existence still speaks today. You just need to learn to tune out all of the other "crazy talk" that bounces inside your head, so you can hear him.

4. It's up to you to start this "conversation" with God. If you don't know how to start, you might read aloud a verse of Scripture that encourages you. If you don't have a specific one, you can read the verse earlier in the chapter that ministered so much to me when Joel Osteen read it on the television. Or you can do as I did and say, "Lord here I am. I'm listening and I trust you to speak to me because I am your sheep. I am your child who needs to hear from you so that I can be lead into all truth. Like Psalm 119 says, I delight in your instruction and ways. Help me to hear you clearly."

5. I encourage you to be open. Some people put limits on God by demanding that he only speak to them with scriptures but I encourage you to remember the patriarchs of the Bible who were communing with God without the benefit of his written word in hand. When we were teaching our children to hear from the Lord, while they were both in elementary school, the first words the Lord spoke to each of them were different. He told my son, that he loved him. He told my daughter that he was proud of her. I'll never forget the joy on their faces. My son said, "Mama, God sounds like my thoughts far away." He is correct. The Lords voice, just as he declares in his word, is a still small voice. In this noisy world, we must tune our

ears to listen. Quietness, faith that he'll speak, and practice are a must.

6. Remember, he's our Father. So, you can and should ask God questions. Something simple, like "Hi, God. Kennisha says you will speak with me. Are you there?"

7. If you've made it this far, now get excited, because God's going to answer you! Yes, the living God is going to answer you. I know you may think it sounds crazy, but trust me. You have to be faithful about this and trust that he's a good God.

   Oh, I'm not saying you're going to hear an audible voice like that of your spouse. But I do believe you will get a thought or an impression. It might sound a lot like your own inner-head voice, but don't discount it.

   Just be still and get ready to write down what you hear.

8. What do you hear? Write it down. Maybe it's just one word. Maybe it's a Bible verse. Maybe it's a sentence. Maybe it sounds like something you need to purchase at the grocery store. No, seriously! Trust me. Just write it down.

9. Now, unless the voice contradicts the Word of God, then I suggest that you are starting to learn to hear from God. Seriously!

   You *are* accountable to validate that it doesn't contradict with the word of God in the Bible, so study your Bible. In my experience, the Holy Spirit is a great teacher. He knows you and where you are in him. His words often bring peace…even if what you receive is a rebuke or correction. So remember common sense. Once I thought I heard the Lord tell me to give something to a person and I wondered if it was the devil. Then I heard the Lord say, why would the enemy tempt you to give. He's a taker. Common Sense!

But anything that speaks to you about how much you are loved, that you have purpose, and that your heavenly Father wants to communicate with you is actually pretty cool!

10. And if you hear that you should go ask forgiveness from someone, that you should stop doing something selfish, or that there might be a wiser person you should talk to, I am thinking that you did not initiate those words to pop into your head at this moment.

11. So, if you're still with me and you know that you heard at least a few words, then write them down. Really! Write them down.

There are a couple of reasons to write down whatever words you hear. If it's really more about your shopping list than saving the entire planet, you want to make sure you have enough milk in the house for tomorrow, now don't you?

But it's also an act of faith. Remember, there is power in being a "doer of the word, not just a hearer." Writing down the words is an act of doing. I suggest that it will encourage you to ask God more questions and for him to keep speaking to you.

Also, you might hear something that sounds completely different than anything you have ever heard before, so you might want to reference it later in your next appointment with God or to share with your spouse.

12. Another option is that you might get a sense of a kind of picture in your mind, instead of specific words. Draw it! That's right, just pretend like you are a trusting 5-year-old child, and draw what you see in your imagination. The Bible speaks about people having visions, and a picture is a kind of vision.

13. And, then again, on the first few tries of hearing from God you might think you didn't hear or see anything except the second hand on your watch counting down the time to the end of this appointment with God. And that's okay, too.

14. Whatever your experience, I encourage you to keep your appointments for the entire week. Don't get discouraged, just be patient and practice your faithfulness. The more you practice being "still and knowing that he is God," the closer you will get to knowing what your God-given purpose is.

I promise: it really works!

Learning to Die to Yourself

Now that Herb and I are living a life of a mature, Christ-centered couple, we are beginning to share our God-given relationship wisdom with people around us. Our teenage son, Trey, is one of those important people we counsel.

Recently, Herb and Trey had an interesting conversation about romantic relationships. Trey had fallen head over heels for a young lady from our church and he wanted to know how best to gain her attention. Curious about his son's true intentions, Herb began with a couple of questions: "Well, son, why do you want her attention? What do you plan to do with it?"

"I just want to spend time with her. I want her to know that I like her."

Understanding male thought processes better than his son, Herb continued his inquiries, "…but to what end? What will you do with her attention?"

Trey answered as a typical teenage boy would: "I guess so we could hang out, play video games, and I could enjoy her company."

Having observed this interaction, I joined the conversation. "Trey why is this so important to you now? You're in the 7th grade. You have plenty of time to spend time with girls. What's the rush?"

To my surprise, he answered, "Well, Mama, I just want what you and daddy have."

At that comment, I answered while laughing, "Aww, sweetie, you have to die to get what we have."

Trey's perplexed young face reflected the confusion within his intelligent mind to what I had just said. I suspect you are also wondering what I meant.

"I assume you mean how close daddy and I are?" I continued with Trey.

"Yes, Ma'am," he responded. "Ya'll are laughing all the time together. I can tell ya'll really like each other, and you always have such fun together."

"Trey, you're right. Dad and I have a lot of fun times together. We have learned to be joyful and to appreciate each other. But, actually, our relationship is the result of a lot of dying.

"I had to die to my wants, will, and ways. And, frankly, it was hard work and it took a lot of time.

"Your daddy also had to die to his personal preferences and desires. He made difficult choices to make our marriage work the way you see it day to day.

"For any couple to gain the unity and joy you see in our relationship requires much effort and commitment from both people. It didn't happen overnight.

So, what you are seeking is not something Dad or I can teach you in a few minutes of conversation so that you might see a short-term change in your friendship with this young lady.

If you truly desire to one day have an amazing marriage like the one that we have, get ready for years of learning to die to yourself."

The Lord promises to give wisdom and direction to anyone who asks him for it. The accessibility to even more of his knowledge is even easier for people who consistently seek it and who actually apply his counsel to their lives. I believe that anyone reading this book is pretty humble, because you are seeking out more information about how to improve your marriage.

After gaining new knowledge, it is important to apply the new concepts into your life. Making these kinds of changes requires even more humility to become a "doer" of what you have learned. Think about it: doing things God's way can be hard on your ego and your desires for self-sufficiency. It is doing something differently than you previously have executed that produces the death to self that I mentioned to my son.

If you have ever had to submit to a manager's preferred method to sweep the floors and take out the trash—even when you know perfectly well how to get the job done—you know what I'm talking about. It can feel very painful to your pride and your self-esteem. Maybe you've even had thoughts like, "Who does she think she is telling me how to use the broom and the dustpan?! I've been keeping my own house clean for the last decade!"

Learning to Die to Yourself

But once you master the way your employer wants you to execute the supposedly simple task, you may find yourself on the receiving end of many good things. Think about it; who gets the promotion from cleaning to cooking at the fast food restaurant? Is it the employee who complains and completes the task half-heartedly using her own methods? Or is it the employee who complies with the procedures and demonstrates a willingness to learn how to adapt?

So, I agree that dying to one's pride, will, and emotions is a painful death, but I want to encourage you that there are benefits. Not only can you gain promotions at work by practicing this type of humility, but I promise that as you and your spouse learn to die to your selves and to each other, there will be plenty of good things to come for you!

If you needed answers to some of the most difficult legal questions and you had legal representation available to you 24x7, would you rely on that lawyer? Or would you ignore the attorney and trust yourself for the answers, even though you're not the expert?

Pride believes it knows everything, while humility seeks out the expert. Concerning marriage and all of life's experiences, God is the expert. Not only is he the creator of all humans, but also he left us a user's manual. The word of God warns us that pride goes before a fall, and even instructs us to buy truth, if necessary (Proverbs 23:23).

Dying to Become One

If we were to cut to the chase, you probably think you need a happy marriage, because misery is too much for any person to bear for too long. So, who are you going to ask for these expert answers?

Herb and I are confident that God takes great delight in marriages. Thousands of years before Jesus Christ entered the world to establish the church and his relationship with it, God created one man for one woman. God created these biblical marriage relationships before all other covenant relationships.

God loves these special unions so much that the Bible records his views on love, courting, marriage, overcoming strife, raising children, and on and on. God is so motivated for marriages to succeed; that he is always willing to provide what is needed for the union to be a happy one. God's ways produce prosperity and wholeness to all who follow them (Deut. 30:16, 32:4). Wisdom also teaches that God wants you to also have a happy marriage.

Actually, God's first words ever spoken to mankind were a blessing over Adam and Eve's marriage: "Be fruitful and multiply!"

God never changes, so it is still his desire for your marriage to be fruitful and multiply. Praise God! God is in your corner. He is pro-marriage!

Now that you know much of the difficult chapters of my life with Herb, I hope you will trust me when I say that we believe in humbly seeking the Lord for everything. Humility is such a key

Learning to Die to Yourself

component of our individual relationships with God, as well as with each other. It may be the most important concept in the foundation of our marriage.

The Lord's instructions are to be humble and seek him for the keys to your marriages success. As you do that, the spirit of understanding will impart into your hearts how to practically walk out the steps. No marriage can get everything from a book, counseling sessions, or your own minds. Marriage is designed to be walked out with the Lord ordering your steps.

As Herb and I were diligent to pray together year after year, we grew more and more humble in each other's presence, especially because we were baring our souls to God in front of the other person. While it may feel awkward in the beginning, this kind of transparency with one another before God is a beautiful thing once you get used to it. I have discovered that it's very difficult to get too high-minded with your spouse over something petty when just a few hours earlier you were praying or weeping with one another at the throne of God.

One of the best benefits, however, is how much easier it is to extend grace and mercy to the other person who consistently hears you asking God for forgiveness for your own shortcomings. Mercy and grace, extended in humility, are powerful components of a loving relationship!

God's word even provides counsel for the person who may be married to someone who hasn't yet realized that his/her marriage can be better. God wants to encourage you, even if your partner might have lost heart for a good marriage, or hasn't yet understood that a happy marriage does not magically appear after saying, "I do." Married life God's way takes consistent effort and much dying to self...even if only one person is willing to start the journey alone to improve the marriage.

Herb and I stopped keeping a record of the couples we've spoken to that were not in agreement about seeking marital assistance. Many couples claim they want to fix their marriage, only to discover in some cases that one or both of them really don't want to do the work to change. Marriage is work.

While it may be easier if both partners are open to working with a counselor, more often only one person is actively seeking for how to improve the marriage. Sometimes the couple is willing to read a book together. Most of my experience seems to be with couples that are willing to seek private advice, even though they are not yet ready to publicly admit their need for marriage insight.

On the other hand, there are individuals who recognize that there is a problem in the marriage, but assume that the source of the problem is the other person. This is NOT a humble attitude! Instead, the accusing person's heart is closing up because of pride that blinds him/her to the fact that two people are involved in the difficult marriage. The really bold and hardened spouses may actually send the other spouse to meet with us to "get fixed."

One day, a neighbor who knew that Herb and I helped couples unexpectedly approached me. This husband boldly crossed

Learning to Die to Yourself

the street to our home and ordered me: "I need you to go to my home and fix my wife! She's acting crazy and our marriage is broken. She needs you."

"No, sir," was my reply. "Your wife needs you! If you want to fix a broken marriage, both of you need to fix it together."

Frankly, each person's primary role in a marriage is to lay down the idea that the other person needs to be "fixed." Instead, learn to study and gain understanding from God's word into your own heart, opening it up for more of God's revelation and growing in more of your God-given humility.

In the beginning, you might find it difficult to discipline yourself to read the Bible or to believe that God really wants to help. I like to say that your heart is like a garden and you might find some rocky soil in there. You might even find a few huge boulders that are blocking your ability to practice more of God's hope, peace, forgiveness, or love. Taking responsibility to begin plowing up the rocky soil of your own heart is a mighty step towards practicing humility and learning to do things differently in your marriage.

In Matthew 7, Jesus used another analogy to explain the responsibility one person has to grow in maturity to God's ways before judging and criticizing someone else. Jesus says to recognize and address the huge piece of wood in your own eye before you start squabbling or fussing about the piece of dust in your partner's eye.

Sure, both of you might have difficulties seeing, but why is it the person with the 2x4 in the eye who is so concerned about sawdust in the other person's eye? God believes it's wiser to focus on your own issues, first, so you can see much more clearly before dealing with someone else's petty issues.

God's word is like a set of tools. For the tool to be applied, at least one person has to pick it up out of the toolbox and start using the tool. But surely you have seen some jobs that are better with two sets of hands. Marriages are always improved when the husband and wife are willing to work together "fixing" the problems.

In the event, however, that your spouse is currently too prideful to pitch in and learn how to use God's tools for your marriage, don't be discouraged. I appreciate that God's ways can still minister into these types of broken marriages. I know that these times can be very disappointing. But don't quit, if you are the spouse that wants change.

Remember, the God of the universe wants you to succeed as an individual and as a covenant partner. If your spouse is not yet ready to work with you on improving your marriage, just lean even more into God's ways and listen for how he will lead you out of the current darkness of your frustrating marriage.

Don't give up! Trust God to reach your spouse and change his/her heart. In the meantime, continue to love your spouse while working on yourself. God's truth teaches about love that never fails!

Learning to Die to Yourself

One of the most important tools in God's toolbox is prayer. Learning to pray God's words over yourself, your spouse, and your marriage will bring more peace and encouragement into your own heart, even while you wait patiently for your spouse to hear God more clearly.

Prayer changes circumstances and hearts, while overcoming pride and egos. Prayer is simply practicing how to listen to God, as I discussed in the previous chapter, plus learning to speak out his word so it can come to pass. Frankly, prayer is a vehicle for learning how his truth serves as a road map for success.

Dying to your own selfish ways of thinking and acting are important in your relationship with God and your spouse. Learning to be humble can feel painful as your pride and thoughts argue with changing your lifetime habits. But be encouraged. God's ways, his words, and your growing relationship with him through prayer will strengthen you, your character, and your relationship with your spouse for a glorious future.

Even if your spouse is not yet ready to walk this path with you, I suggest you practice the following activities as you learn to use God's special tools for your life. Believe me when I say that God's blessings will begin to show so that your spouse and other people will begin to see the new you emerging!

Learning to Practice Humility

Check your own heart

Is your heart open to new revelation from God about your marriage? Are you prepared to obey? The condition of your heart must be open to receive a word from the Lord about your character and your situation.

Take the time at your next few appointments with God to examine yourself. Answer these questions honestly, allowing for spontaneous responses to appear in your quiet time. Consider such questions as these:

1. Am I open to change?
2. Can God really speak to my heart and expect me to listen?
3. Am I open to correction and conviction from the Holy Spirit?
4. Do I already know the answers to my marriage issues?
5. When reading this book, what feelings stir up in me?
6. Is there any unrepentant sin in my life? Am I guilty of not being truthful, kind, or obedient to God or my spouse? If so, be transparent with God and ask his forgiveness. Do you need to ask the forgiveness of your spouse?
7. Am I prompted in my inner self to go forward or run?

Now take your answers and think them over. What do they say about you? Do you want to run away? Or are you motivated to go forward learning whatever God has set aside for you?

Learning to Die to Yourself

Feeding your heart

So how do you prepare you own heart? Humble yourself. Humility is the key to receiving anything from the Lord.

The firmest foundation of true humility comes from the recognition that God is smarter, wiser, kinder, and more loving than you are. And, yet, his goal is to enable you to continue to grow into more and more of the holy, joyful, and wise image that Jesus, as the son of God, demonstrated when walking on this earth as a human.

Seem impossible? Of course it is! At least until you are willing to learn how God wants you to mature.

The first step of growing in humility and becoming more like Jesus is to recognize what God says about you in each area of your life. The Bible provides the time-tested, wise counsel of the creator of the universe. As you read scripture aloud, your mind will begin to mature. Personalizing God's promises reinforce the concepts to retrain your thoughts and your actions.

I suggest you pray these scriptures in your prayer time. Just add yourself into God's word by personalizing them. Below each scripture, I've included examples of how I have personalized God's wisdom for my own use.

The rewards of humility and the reverence of the Lord are riches, honor, and life. Proverbs 22:4

Father, I pray that you'd reward my marriage with humility and reverence of the Lord, which bring riches, honor, and life, in the name of Jesus.

Lord, you have heard the desire and the longing of the humble; you will prepare and strengthen and direct their heart, you will cause your ear to hear. Psalms 10:17

Lord, you have heard the desire and longing of my humble heart. Thank you for preparing and strengthening and directing my heart and my spouse's heart and causing us to have ears to hear from you.

Yea, all of you be subject to one another, and be clothed with humility; for God resists the proud and give grace to the humble. 1 Peter 5:5

Father, in the name of Jesus, I pray that you'd teach me/us to be subject to one another, clothing us with humility. We receive the grace you give to the humble. Thank you Lord.

Now, you practice personalizing God's words into your own life.

Love is patient, love is kind, love has no envy, love has no opinion of itself, love has no pride. Love's ways are fair, it takes no thought for itself, it is not quickly made angry, it takes no record of wrongs done to it, it takes no pleasure in wrongdoings, but has joy in what is true. Love has the power of undergoing all things, having faith in all things, hoping in all things. Though

Learning to Die to Yourself

the prophet's word may come to an end, tongues come to nothing, and even knowledge has no more value, love never fails. 1 Corinthians 13:4 – 8

_____
_____
_____
_____
_____
_____
_____
_____
_____
_____

What other scriptures or inspiring sentences can you personalize and start declaring over your life and your marriage?

Use your Bible or the search features of a Bible website or application, searching for whatever word speaks strongest to your heart.

_____

_____

_____

By seeking God's ways in another area of your life, you are demonstrating your willingness to be trained by him. And you are practicing your growing humility. Keep it up!

Trusting the process

As you start speaking out the scriptures in a personal manner, you may start to have thoughts that challenge you. On one hand, you might actually want to allow your spouse's preferences to direct your next date night, rather than argue that you want to go to your favorite restaurant. Congratulations! Even if it feels uncomfortable to allow someone else to orchestrate your steps, it might be fun. I also suspect that your willingness to be more gentle and humble will strengthen your relationship.

On the other hand, I have also experienced receiving lots of criticism, either from other people or in my own head. For example, I have heard words accusing me that I wasn't truly humble, and that I was a liar for speaking out that I am humble. Congratulations! You must be on the right path with God when these types of accusations appear.

Learning to Die to Yourself

I assure you it is very normal for other people to challenge your commitment to shift your thinking to align with God's perspective of you. They may want to test your sincerity to change, or even try to derail your efforts to improve yourself. Remember, God operates by faith, speaking out the desired result even before anyone can see it. That's what you're doing, learning to talk like God and to mature in his ways.

So, hear me clearly: You're not lying! Instead, it's as if you're painting a picture of your future self with words. And it's an awesome result if you'll not stop speaking his good words over your life!

Whatever discomfort you might feel as you learn to speak God's scriptures in a personal manner, don't stop! The discomfort and insecurity will disappear the more you demonstrate consistency. I use the analogy that learning to speak God's words is just like learning to train for a 5K race. Yes, the first couple of weeks you might feel sore or foolish. But soon thereafter your body actually starts to crave the training. And, if you choose to continue the new exercise program, soon you're running across the finish line!

Remember, you can do this. God is no respecter of persons, so his process works as well for you as for me as long as you trust him. Just be diligent, don't quit, and remember that I'm praying for your glorious marriage.

You've got this!

Dying to Become One

Learning the Power of Grace and Mercy

No healthy person needs a doctor; doctors are for sick people. It is the same with marriages: most couples don't seek help until something is broken. Just like a physical ailment, though, once a few areas of your married life are broken, it seems that everything starts breaking down. Have you ever noticed that, or wondered why it occurs that way?

Often in times of counseling a couple, Herb and I easily recognize the pattern of a pattern of a spouse who accuses that the other person <u>always</u> does this or that. Or, at times, Herb and I can't tell if the couple fighting about something current or something that happened years ago, because the details become vague and everything seems muddled together.

When you and your spouse have disagreements, do you actual resolve the issue and forgive one another? Or do you ignore the problem and allow the unresolved hurts to fester like an emotional cancer?

The kingdom of God works on a strict set of spiritual laws, just as with the natural realm. In nature, gravity is working all the time. You can try to convince yourself that you can fly like a bird, but what happens when a person jumps off a roof? Gravity is always present, isn't it?

The same is true with God's grace and mercy. Because God is love, he created the earth to foster gentleness, kindness, and forgiveness. Can you imagine how great it would have been to live with Adam and Eve in the Garden of Eden? Hope, patience, and joy were always present.

That is, God's goodness was all encompassing on the earth until the human emotions of fear, envy, jealousy, and rebellion entered the scene. Rather than trusting God enough to ask him if they could eat of the forbidden fruit, Adam and Eve chose their own, selfish path to use their free will and openly disobey his commandment to leave that one tree's fruit alone. And, just as there is a natural consequence of gravity, there is a spiritual consequence of disobeying God: his peace and his goodness must step aside from human selfishness.

Even today, God's spiritual laws operate with consistency. God draws closer when a person operates in faith, hope, and peace. And, while never abandoning his child, God's peace and presence are not as tangible when that person chooses to demonstrate strife, anger, or other selfish behaviors. God is a generous parent, but he will <u>not</u> participate in child-like temper tantrums. Instead, I envision God standing patiently at the sideline

Learning the Power of Grace and Mercy

waiting for the child to realize that she's ready to receive comfort and wisdom from him, rather than to rudely demand her way with the people around her.

The Bible refers to the works of the flesh in contrast to the fruit of the Spirit in Galatians Chapter 5. Anything that is not pleasing to God and his ways are considered sin. Based on my experiences as a wife and an adviser, two of the most common sins that infest marriages are un-forgiveness and the lack of repentance—or apologizing and changing the behaviors—for any sinful act. Frankly, according to Romans 6:23, sin of any sort brings the spiritual consequence of "death," to an individual or to a marriage. As with Adam and Eve, the death may not be immediately physical, but I assure you that God's peace and presence will feel like they are walking away from you: it's a spiritual law.

Un-forgiveness and being unrepentant are like cancers to your marriage: they grow and push out all the vital nutrients in your marriage like trust, joy, and even love. Un-forgiveness and being unrepentant also stop the flow of grace and mercy in your life, and open the door to allow a flood of torment, strife, and confusion to exist.

So, I challenge you to consider your own marriage. Do you see more "fruit" of kindness, love, grace, and mercy? Or more "works" of torment, strife, un-forgiveness, or confusion?

I suggest that practicing grace and mercy will overcome any sinful works that try to creep into your marriage. Jesus gives a great example of why you should give grace and mercy to another person. In Matthew 18:21-35, Jesus tells the story of a ruler who forgives a debtor all of his debts. The ruler gives grace and mercy to the debtor, when the ruler could have legally have sold the debtor into slavery or killed him for the crime of unpaid debts. Which would you prefer: to be forgiven by grace and mercy, or killed for your unpaid debts?

Jesus continues the story by explaining how the debtor then has the opportunity to extend the same grace to other people who owed money to the forgiven debtor. Rather than being kind and gracious, however, the forgiven debtor throws another person into jail for his unpaid debts. What?! It seems pretty rude to me. What do you think about this forgiven debtor's behavior?

In Jesus' story, the forgiving ruler was so upset by the actions of the forgiven debtor, that the ruler was actually "grieved." But the ruler didn't stop there, with a heavy heart. Instead, the kind and generous king realized that the forgiven debtor was negatively impacting all kinds of people around him, so the ruler delivered the forgiven debtor "into the hands of the tormentors." Think about it: the graceful king tried to protect the debtor from his own, unwise actions that produced the unpaid debts. In response, the forgiven debtor chose to be selfish and unkind to other people. As a consequence of the spiritual laws of God, the forgiven debtor ended up living with much torment. I would prefer to be pleasing to the ways of God than live in torment. How about you?

The benefits of grace and mercy reach deeper than just forgiving a financial debt. Grace and mercy are actually the foundation of God's personality and the reason that Jesus came to the earth as a baby. God values grace and mercy so much that he gave his only son Jesus, so that each person might choose to live free of condemnation, torment, guilt, and the other consequences of selfish behaviors.

God's grace and mercy is a free gift to anyone who receives it. Frankly, it's the heart of the good news of Jesus. I like an explanation I once heard on the radio: God loves you; will you let him help you?

So, the lesson I take away is that because Jesus loves me and died on the cross for all of my past sins—some of which I have openly shared with you—I seek to reflect God's grace and mercy to every person I meet. Of course, there are days when I am less patient or less wise. I <u>am</u> still human, right?

But I have made the decision that once I realize that I have been unforgiving, or rude, or thoughtless to the people around me, I then take action to correct my course of action. First, I ask forgiveness of God. Then I ask him the best way to correct my sinful action with the appropriate people. Sometimes I just ask forgiveness and apologize to my spouse or my children. Sometimes I write a note or offer to serve the offended person in a way that is meaningful to them. Mostly, however, I just learn to trust that God will teach me how and when to address the issue and continue to improve my own character flaws, so that the next time I'm tired or hungry I can dig deeper inside and choose to be kinder to the people whom I love so much.

Now, I'm not naïve. I know that dying to my own preferences or selfish actions is not easy! But I have also learned that I would rather humble myself in asking forgiveness of someone else so that I can grow in my maturity in God than have to humble myself to the same person for the same behavior time and time again. Some days I may be a slower student than other days, but I do eventually "get" it.

Mostly, however, this process of receiving and giving grace reinforces the wisest choice of all: to lean on, trust in, and rely up upon the Lord Jesus Christ for each and every action. He really does know best! And my current life reinforces to me daily how thankful I am to have taken the time to lay down my pride and sinful ways to walk with Jesus every day.

Practically, the steps to forgiving and repenting are easy, but learning to exercise it is not always easy. Let me walk you through an example to show you more specifically how to forgive and repent.

Learning the Power of Grace and Mercy

Imagine that you suspect your spouse is cheating on you. I know that this is an emotional scenario. Your first reaction might be to throw the spouse out of the house with all of his/her belongings. Your family might even support you in that task. But just slow down a bit and see what God says.

From my experience, infidelity may be more a symptom of a root cause in the marriage relationship rather than an out-and-out rejection of a spouse's desire to stay married to you. Personally, because God is so faithful in his covenant to me, I don't believe the suspicion or even the first instance of unfaithfulness is grounds for divorce. Instead, I would hope to understand if/how the marriage could be restored to be even better than before if both people are willing to communicate and consider living closer to God's best in their marriage.

First of all, take your situation to God. Just as you have been practicing with your daily appointments with God, get quiet and then tell him what the situation is. Like in King David's Psalms, feel free to pour all of your anger and hurt and disappointment into the lap of your Father God who cares for you. Just remember, however, that you don't want to stay in a state of self-pity or anger, because they will keep God's peace further from you than you want. Instead, over time, figure out the logic of the situation and ask God for his wisdom as to how to address the situation.

If we imagine that the husband has cheated on the wife, then there are several choices to be made. Will the husband confess and repent, and will the wife forgive? Both of these people have choices to make. Even if the husband does not initiate the revelation of the infidelity, will he acknowledge his sinful and selfish behaviors that wounded his bride to whom he had committed his life?

Repentance is the term I use to reflect the sincere apology of a sinful act such that new behaviors are developed. Apologizing to your spouse is appropriate and beneficial for the offended party, but the value of repentance is that it actually lays the groundwork for your own change. In this example, a repentant husband is acknowledging his intentions to change and his willingness to learn how to change to make his current marriage stronger.

The act of repentance is a spiritual act that can only truly occur by the spirit of God's humility working within the person. As with all behaviors and communications, you can learn to assess the sincerity of a person's repentance. What do you hear? Is the apology full of excuses and justifications? If so, the unfaithful spouse is operating in more pride than in true humility.

On the other hand, do you hear transparent communication that indicates the person is willing to listen to your opinion and practice different behaviors? Do you feel hopeful and peaceful that you and your spouse will be able to work through the difficulties with the grace of God? Then that sounds like a humble and sincere repentance with which you two can move forward.

Be encouraged. The apostle John encourages the church in First John Chapter 5 that Jesus is faithful and just to forgive us when we repent. By the grace of God, realize that God is quick to hear and forgive a repentant heart. He loves you that much!

Frankly, however, the more difficult decision is whether the wife will forgive the husband's unfaithfulness. Now, I'm not saying the wife needs to be a passive doormat and allow her husband to sleep with anyone he wants. That's not healthy for anyone! What I am asking is, will the wife dig down deep into her heart and remember all of her own shortcomings that God has forgiven her, and at least be willing to work through the issues with her spouse? Some people believe it actually takes more spiritual strength to forgive than to repent.

The second challenge, however, is to learn how to forgive and allow God to heal your heart. Just as the wife, in this instance, can choose to give grace and forgiveness to the man she loved enough to marry, she needs to ensure that she is drawing on more of God's grace than ever before. Praying and asking the Lord to help you forgive your spouse is an important step in this healing process.

Then forgive the repentant spouse by grace. Literally, say the words, "By grace I forgive my spouse for ___." Realize, however, that forgiveness is not a benefit for the hurtful person. To reinforce the benefit of forgiving, I remember an analogy of un-forgiveness: it's like drinking poison and expecting the <u>other</u> person to die. Instead, as you forgive another person, the process cleanses <u>your</u> heart, so that you can hear more clearly from the Lord. As soon as you forgive, you will once again be reminded of Jesus' saving grace for you.

Frankly, whether or not you forgive is not based on your standard of right or wrong. On the contrary, Jesus taught the disciples to forgive every time they began to pray and realized that they had anything against someone else. God set the standard, and Jesus commanded the wisest path to obtain God's best (Mark 11:25).

Forgiveness also lays the foundation for your own emotional healing. Ask God to help you heal and bring restoration to what has been broken. Remember, Jesus came to heal the broken-hearted; he wants to help you heal, if you'll let him. While Jesus can heal hearts miraculously, it is more common that emotional healing can take months or even years.

Please don't confuse extending forgiveness with receiving healing, because they are not the same. As a loving parent, I immediately forgive my children of their wrongdoings, because it's easy for me to do: they are after all my children. Despite the ease

Learning the Power of Grace and Mercy

of forgiving my children, I still make them accountable for the appropriate consequence for their actions, just as I learned from my mama's disciplinary actions.

There have been times, however, when what my loving children have done was so hurtful and dishonorable, that I was unable to address the situation in a mature and loving manner. Instead, before I handed out their punishments, I had to calm down or heal. If I hadn't taken the time to regain my composure, frankly, I would have exerted selfish and vengeful retribution because of my wounded heart, rather than wise and loving consequences.

Dealing with a wounded heart within a married couple is at least as complex as a mother wisely dealing with her children. So, remember to practice patience and regroup before saying or doing anything to your spouse that you might learn to regret.

The Lord desires to bless marriages. He wants to give grace and mercy and he loves supporting couples that are willing and able to learn how to repent, forgive, and give grace and mercy. Remember that humility understands that only God can save a marriage, only his ways will work, and he can't fail. God is also large enough that he can save any marriage where the two people will choose to learn how to do things his ways.

On the other hand, if you know that your marriage has areas of unrepentant sin and areas where you haven't forgiven each other, it's time to fix it. Realize that God's peace and presence will not be as tangible within your marriage if either of you is unwilling to repent or forgive. It's not that God is holding out on you, it's that his spiritual law cannot be circumvented.

Recognize that God is holy. He is righteous and just in all his ways. Furthermore, God is light and there is no darkness in him, and his face is against those who do evil. Therefore, people who refuse to repent or forgive are like the forgiven debtor who chose not to pass along mercy and grade to other people.

It's as if Jesus can only be as gracious and merciful to a person as that person is to other people, once the Lord has revealed these concepts to him/her. I do not want the Lord to turn me over to my tormentors when he has grace available for me, as the ruler did in Jesus' story. Do you?

When the two of you are ready to proceed through the difficulties--such as the example of infidelity—within your marriage with repentant and forgiving hearts, write down any area of resentment you still feel towards your spouse or your marriage. The goal of this step, and the next few steps, is to expose the hidden dark spots of your marriage that are hindering the two of you from becoming the "one" that God intends for you. As you choose to allow love to move you forward through this exercise, God will help you see your marriage through to a hopeful end.

Learning the Power of Grace and Mercy

Remember how I shared that sometimes Herb and I wonder if a couple is arguing about today's issues with taking out the trash or fussing about the garbage from three years ago? This is where you need to make the time as individuals to at least identify to yourself all of the past issues that cross your mind each time you feel insecure, dishonored, or ignored in your marriage.

Next, as individuals, write down any areas of guilt, condemnation, or conviction you feel. What do you wish you had done better in times past? How might you have contributed to the negative issues that always seem to live right beneath the surface in your home?

This willingness to identify your own shortcomings is another important step in dying to yourself and learning to live a life of humility. Of course it would be inappropriate for your husband to be sleeping with another woman, but is there a possibility that he felt dishonored by your treatment of him in public? Is it possible that your focus on your professional responsibilities communicated that he was not the most important person in your life?

Be real and honest as you take the time to see your behaviors from his point of view. Be bold enough to ask God to help you see and remember things that your selfish ways blinded to you in your past choices and behaviors. Believe me, I know this isn't fun or pretty, but there is value to you and to your marriage to walk through this step with God.

Once the two of you have written down your resentments and guilty feelings, share them with one another. Listen to each other without interruptions or quick judgments. Practice the patience and gentleness that God promises. As you work through one item at a time, realize how <u>both</u> of you inadvertently contributed to the difficult memory.

Did you not fully understand the emotional state of your spouse because of his/her upbringing or assumptions when you insisted that you must have your way about how to manage the household finances? Did you not realize that your spouse's passive "whatever" response was a defensive coping mechanism to cover his/her own wounded childhood heart, rather than permission for you to enroll in graduate school? Did you not clearly realize that your spouse's insecurities about raising children was affecting not only his/her responsibilities at home, but also at the office?

Are you willing to open your hearts and share the deep hurts and guilt with the person you supposedly love the most in the whole world? Like an abandoned home, it takes the two of you to allow it to fall into disrepair or to choose to restore it to a beautiful and glorious state where you, your family, and your friends enjoy visiting. The choice is yours.

As the two of you choose to be transparent with one another, recognize that the next step is to repent and forgive one another for those past hurts and weaknesses. I doubt that either of you ever intended to be thoughtless, shallow, or selfish.

Unfortunately, however, those character weaknesses are more and more common in contemporary society.

Forgiveness is a gift. Practice giving and receiving it graciously. No, it may not feel comfortable in the beginning, but keep at it. It gets easier, I promise!

But also remember that because forgiveness is a gift, no one should have to work off your forgiveness. What work did you do to earn Jesus' forgiveness? And, remember, that once it's forgiven neither of you should use it as guilt or ammunition for a future disagreement.

To encourage you that this process of learning to give and receive mercy and grace works, I want to share an example of a couple who decided to actually work through this difficult exercise. It truly blessed their marriage!

Ron and Melissa

Ron and Melissa had a good marriage of ten years, but they wanted it to be better. They noticed that they were not as connected as they had once been. When they did the above exercise, they found that they didn't have anything to repent for, but they had many unspoken resentments. Upon analyzing their perspectives, Ron and Melissa realized that all of their resentments were connected to money.

As an example, Melissa resented Ron for not making more money than she did. When she expressed this perspective, Ron shared that he resented himself, as well. Melissa was shocked at his low self-opinion! And then Melissa was saddened, because she knew he was always a diligent worker; she didn't like knowing that the man she loved had been in such turmoil.

In talking out the issue, Ron further explained that he felt limited that he would never be able to make more money without getting his bachelor's degree. On some levels, Ron resented the fact that Melissa had already earned her college degree. Ron's jealousy and insecurity clouded his perceptions, making him fearful that Melissa would never consider supporting their household if he were to enroll in school to finish his degree. These were difficult conversations for Ron and Melissa. Not only did the process challenge their views of marriage roles and breadwinning, but also their views of each person through their own eyes and those of their spouse.

After much discussion, Ron and Melissa decided that the only real solution was for Ron to go back to school and get his degree. While there would be a couple of leans years with only one income, overcoming those financial challenges would be better than a continued lifetime of resentments. Melissa could be excited that Ron was positioning himself as the financial head of the household; to support her emotional security needs, while Ron's self-esteem began to improve. In addition, the perceived trust and

Learning the Power of Grace and Mercy

faithfulness of each spouse for the other person began to heal and mature.

By taking the time to reflect and share their deepest thoughts and emotions, Ron and Melissa found a wise and supportive solution to overcome the primary source of their marriage's weaknesses.

You, too, can initiate healing in your home, like Ron and Melissa. Go for it! Remember, you need each other to build an amazing, godly marriage. And, as you choose to lay down your selfish choices and to trust God's loving ways, you will truly see that love conquers all!

Meditating on Grace and Mercy

Just as you practiced in the previous chapter, there is value in meditating and speaking out personalized versions of God's word. Here are two scriptures to reinforce the fact that life with God as individuals and as couples is a journey: we have to choose to leave the past in the past and to continue on towards the future with Jesus, leaving all guilt and condemnation at the foot of the cross each time we repent and forgive.

I do not consider, brothers, that I have captured and made it my own way (yet), but one thing I do know, forgetting what lies behind and straining forward to what lies ahead, I press toward the goal to win the prize to which God in Christ Jesus is calling us upward. So let those of us who are spiritually mature and full-grown have this mind and hold these convictions; and if any respect you have a different attitude of mind, God will make that clear to you also. Only let us hold true to what we have already attained and walk and order our lives by that. Philippians 3:13 – 16

There is therefore now no condemnation to them which are in Christ Jesus, who walk not after the flesh, but after the Spirit. Roman 8:1

Postscript

*For this cause shall a man leave his father and mother
and shall be joined unto his wife, and they two shall be one flesh.
This is a great mystery; but I speak concerning Christ and the church.
Ephesians 5:31-32*

Our Bible is filled with the expressions of true unity. From the beginning, we find Adam surrounded and filled with perfection but still longing for companionship. God fulfilled his desire with Eve. A woman made just for him. With their union, Adam and Eve changed the planet forever.

Never again has the Lord had to take from the man to create his woman, but the joining of two is still the same. God still delights in giving us companionship. Our unions express love, unity, and wholeness like nothing else in the earth. We express the nature of God when we live in harmony together. A Christian marriage is also the best expression of Christ's unity with his church—each one of us. This is the greatest mystery of all!

The success of our marriages has a far greater impact in the earth and the spirit realm than the enemy would like for us to understand. He would like for each of us to be ignorant of our impact on the world with the simplicity of our daily lives. For a moment, the serpent's scheme deceived Adam and Eve as well. We could all be living in the Garden of Eden if Adam and Even had worked together to keep the devil and his selfish ways out of their lives.

Praise God for Jesus who has given each of us another chance to make better decisions!

If we allow the destruction of the unity in our homes, we can't be used to bring unity and love to the world. Through unity, we demonstrate the full measure of Jesus Christ (Ephesian 4:3,13). This demonstration of Christ who is love, joy, peace, patience, gentleness, goodness, faith, humility, and temperance will change whatever and whomever we chose to engage. In essence, we will be the salt that Jesus instructed us to become.

Many people have tried to save the world with grandiose plans while neglecting the management of their homes. But this, my friend, is out of order. How can we reach out to the world, but not have time to bless our own families? Our first ministry is at home. From that loving place, we can create a platform for success in everything else we face.

Since my journey with this book began, my own marriage has grown and in many regards become a new union. While my husband and I reread my original words from six years ago, we were both convicted on different levels by some of the practices we haven't taken for granted. The writing of this book has renewed and revised us. It's brought new passion to our union and for that I'm grateful.

Postscript

I include these words because I've learned over the last twenty years that marriage is indeed a journey. It's similar to building a house, moving into it, and then the real work of maintenance begins. Those who diligently maintain their homes increase the value of it and despite its age, it stands as a testimony of quality craftsmanship, excellence in maintenance, and a love of history and legacy. People will marvel as it majesty and its ability to stand the test of time.

I hope you as a reader, if you don't take anything else from this book that you walk away understanding that the great mystery of marriage is the sacrifice that two people must make to truly love, accept, and strengthen each other. With God's grace and his leading, all things are possible. Don't fear; believe only.

I encourage you in your marriages and the challenges you face. The Lord is on your side. And His word is your guide to how marriage should work. No humble prayer goes unanswered. Routine checks of your grace and mercy are necessary.

Just as you can talk to God about everything, talk to your spouse, too...about everything. Keep the lines of honest communication open.

And, finally, know who you are in Christ so that you can truly live for him, shine for him, and bring change in your home and in the earth for him.

God bless you all. I pray that you've been blessed and changed by the words I've shared with you. I pray for wholeness for every family who has humbly read this book, in the name of Jesus!

Kennisha Moffett

Bibliography

Great Marriage Books (Other than the Bible)

1. Men Are from Mars, Women Are from Venus

   Book by John Gray

2. Men Are Like Waffles — Women Are Like Spaghetti

   Book by Pam Farrel and Bill Farrel

3. The 5 Languages of Love by Gary Chapman

4. His Needs, Her Needs by Willard F. Jr. Harley

5. The Power of a Praying Wife by Stormie Omartian

6. The Purpose and Power of Love & Marriage by Dr. Myles Munroe

7. Keys for Marriage by Dr. Myles Munroe

8. Understanding the Purpose and Power of Prayer by Dr. Myles Munroe

Movies & Websites

1. Fireproof Movie

2. The Notebook Movie

3. http://www.fireproofmymarriage.com/

4. http://www.focusonthefamily.com/marriage/articles/marriage_ministry.aspx
5. http://www.crosswalk.com/family/marriage/
6. http://www.lifeway.com/n/Christian-Living/Marriage-&-Relationships?type=learn
7. http://www.cbn.com/family/Marriage/

www.ingramcontent.com/pod-product-compliance
Lightning Source LLC
Chambersburg PA
CBHW070316240426
43661CB00057B/2658